Pi Network: Breaking Crypto Ground

Pioneer Peter

Published by Pioneer Peter, 2023.

While every precaution has been taken in the preparation of this book, the publisher assumes no responsibility for errors or omissions, or for damages resulting from the use of the information contained herein.

PI NETWORK: BREAKING CRYPTO GROUND

First edition. July 30, 2023.

ISBN: 979-8223914228

Written by Pioneer Peter.

PI NETWORK BREAKING CRYPTO GROUND

Seizing Opportunities Beyond Mining For Success

By

Pioneer Peter

Copyright Page:

Title: Pi Network: Breaking Crypto Ground

Author: Pioneer Peter

© 2023 by Pioneer Peter

Disclaimer: The information provided in this book is intended for general knowledge purposes only and does not constitute financial or investment advice. The author and publisher of this book are not financial advisors, and the content presented here should not be considered as a substitute for professional financial consultation. Readers are encouraged to seek advice from a qualified financial professional before making any investment decisions or financial commitments.

While the author and publisher have made every effort to ensure the accuracy and completeness of the information provided in this book, they do not warrant or guarantee its correctness or suitability for any particular purpose. The information in this book is subject to change without notice and may not be current or up-to-date at the time of reading.

The author and publisher disclaim any liability for any financial loss or damage arising directly or indirectly from the use of the information presented in this book. Readers are solely responsible for their own investment decisions and should exercise caution and due diligence before taking any action based on the content of this book.

References to specific financial products, services, or companies are for illustrative purposes only and do not constitute endorsements or recommendations.

For permission requests, please contact the publisher at. gmcooilco@gmail.com

This book is dedicated to:

To All Those Disfranchised by the Centralized Financial System,

This book is dedicated to you, the resilient souls who have faced barriers and limitations within the centralized financial system. You are the ones who have struggled against unequal access, unfair practices, and exclusion from the opportunities that should rightfully belong to all.

Your perseverance in the face of adversity has inspired us to shed light on the imbalances and advocate for a more inclusive and equitable financial landscape. Your experiences have fueled our passion to challenge the status quo and seek a better future for everyone.

In a world where the centralized financial system has left many behind, your determination to overcome these challenges serves as a beacon of hope. You are the driving force behind our mission to dismantle barriers and open doors for all to partake in the prosperity that the financial world has to offer.

May this book be a tribute to your resilience and a testament to our shared vision for a financial system that empowers and uplifts every individual, regardless of their background or circumstances.

With deep gratitude and unwavering commitment,
Pioneer Peter
Pi Network: Breaking Crypto Ground

Part I: Introduction To Cryptocurrency World:

Chapter 1: Introduction to Cryptocurrencies:

IN THIS UNIT, WE WILL embark on an exhilarating journey into the world of cryptocurrencies, where the financial landscape is undergoing a profound transformation. We will delve into the core concepts and fascinating history behind cryptocurrencies, exploring their impact on our global economy.

Cryptocurrency is a digital or virtual form of currency that uses cryptography for secure financial transactions, control the creation of additional units, and verify the transfer of assets. It is a decentralized form of currency that operates on a technology called blockchain, which is a distributed ledger that records all transactions across a network of computers.

Alternative words or terms for cryptocurrency include:

1. Digital currency
2. Virtual currency
3. Crypto
4. Cryptoasset
5. Token
6. Digital asset
7. Electronic money
8. Cybercurrency
9. Altcoin (referring to alternative cryptocurrencies other than Bitcoin)

10. Digital tokens

These alternative words and terms are often used interchangeably to refer to the broader category of digital currencies that employ cryptographic techniques for secure transactions.

1. What are cryptocurrencies?

- Imagine a digital realm where money flows freely, unencumbered by the traditional banking system. Cryptocurrencies are precisely that - digital or virtual currencies that utilize cryptography for secure transactions, independent of central authorities like banks or governments.

- Cryptocurrencies operate on decentralized networks, relying on innovative technologies to facilitate peer-to-peer transactions, store value, and enable new applications.

2. Brief history of cryptocurrencies:

- To truly appreciate the significance of cryptocurrencies, we need to grasp their humble beginnings. We will trace the origins back to the enigmatic Satoshi Nakamoto, the pseudonymous creator of Bitcoin, the first and most renowned cryptocurrency.

Let's delve into the key milestones and significant events that have shaped the cryptocurrency landscape, highlighting the emergence of alternative cryptocurrencies (altcoins) and the growing acceptance of blockchain technology:

1. Emergence of Bitcoin: In 2009, Bitcoin was introduced as the first decentralized cryptocurrency by the pseudonymous figure known as Satoshi Nakamoto. This event marked the beginning of a transformative era, where individuals could transact directly without intermediaries and with enhanced privacy and security.

2. Rise of Altcoins: Following the success of Bitcoin, alternative cryptocurrencies, often referred to as altcoins, began to emerge. Litecoin (2011) introduced faster transaction confirmations, while Ripple (2012) aimed to revolutionize cross-border payments. Ethereum (2015) played a significant role by introducing smart contracts, enabling the creation

of decentralized applications (dApps) and paving the way for a wave of innovation.

3. Initial Coin Offerings (ICOs): Around 2017, Initial Coin Offerings gained prominence as a crowdfunding method for cryptocurrency startups. ICOs allowed companies to raise funds by selling tokens, often built on the Ethereum blockchain, in exchange for cryptocurrencies like Bitcoin or Ether. This fundraising mechanism enabled the rapid growth of blockchain projects and the diversification of the cryptocurrency ecosystem.

4. Mainstream Adoption and Acceptance: Over time, cryptocurrencies and blockchain technology gained wider acceptance and recognition. Major companies, including Microsoft, Dell, and Expedia, started accepting Bitcoin as a form of payment. Additionally, financial institutions such as JPMorgan and Fidelity began exploring blockchain applications for their operations. This growing acceptance by established players validated the potential of cryptocurrencies and their underlying technology.

5. Regulatory Developments: The cryptocurrency landscape witnessed increasing regulatory scrutiny and efforts to provide legal frameworks. Various countries implemented regulations to address concerns like anti-money laundering (AML) and investor protection. Governments also explored the concept of central bank digital currencies (CBDCs) as a way to leverage the benefits of cryptocurrencies while maintaining regulatory control.

6. Blockchain Use Cases Beyond Cryptocurrencies: The potential of blockchain technology extended beyond cryptocurrencies. Industries such as supply chain management, healthcare, voting systems, and decentralized finance (DeFi) began exploring blockchain's transparent and immutable nature for increased efficiency, security, and trust.

7. Cryptocurrency Market Volatility: The cryptocurrency market experienced significant volatility, with sharp price fluctuations and market cycles. These fluctuations were influenced by factors like market

speculation, regulatory announcements, technological advancements, and macroeconomic events. Understanding the volatile nature of the cryptocurrency market became crucial for investors and participants.

These milestones and events collectively shaped the cryptocurrency landscape, demonstrating the disruptive potential of cryptocurrencies and the transformative power of blockchain technology. From the introduction of Bitcoin as the pioneer to the rise of altcoins, ICOs, and the exploration of blockchain use cases, the cryptocurrency ecosystem has evolved significantly, impacting various industries and garnering increased mainstream attention.

3. Key concepts: blockchain, decentralization, and cryptography:

- Blockchain: Picture a virtual ledger that records all cryptocurrency transactions across a network of computers. This distributed ledger, known as the blockchain, is the foundation of cryptocurrencies. We will examine its immutable and transparent nature, understanding how it ensures the integrity of transactions and fosters trust in the system.

- Decentralization: In a world dominated by centralized institutions, decentralization revolutionizes the way we perceive trust and authority. We will uncover the power of decentralized networks, where consensus mechanisms and peer validation ensure the security and stability of cryptocurrencies.

- Cryptography: Encryption lies at the heart of cryptocurrencies, shielding transactions and wallets from prying eyes. We will demystify the cryptographic techniques employed, such as public-key cryptography and digital signatures, to safeguard privacy and secure the integrity of the blockchain.

Cryptography and Blockchain Makes Cryptocurrency Secure and Transparent

Cryptography:

Cryptography is the practice of securing communication by converting information into a format that is unintelligible to unauthorized individuals, known as ciphertext. It involves the use of mathematical algorithms and cryptographic keys to encrypt and decrypt data, ensuring its confidentiality, integrity, and authenticity.

Let's take a simple example to understand cryptography better: the Caesar cipher. In this ancient encryption technique, each letter in a message is shifted a certain number of positions down the alphabet. For instance, if we shift each letter three positions down, "HELLO" becomes "KHOOR." To decrypt the message, the recipient would shift each letter three positions up to retrieve the original text.

In modern cryptography, more complex algorithms are used, such as the Advanced Encryption Standard (AES) or the Rivest-Shamir-Adleman (RSA) algorithm. These algorithms use longer keys and more sophisticated mathematical operations, making them highly secure and virtually impossible to break without the corresponding decryption key.

Blockchain:

Blockchain is a decentralized, transparent, and immutable digital ledger that records all transactions across a network of computers. It is a foundational technology behind cryptocurrencies like Bitcoin and Ethereum, but its applications extend beyond digital currencies.

To understand blockchain, let's imagine a simple scenario: a group of friends lending and borrowing money among themselves. Traditionally, they would rely on a central authority, like a bank, to keep track of these transactions. However, in a blockchain-based system, the friends create a shared ledger, or the "blockchain," where all transactions are recorded.

Whenever a transaction occurs, it is grouped with other transactions into a "block." Each block contains a unique identifier, a timestamp, and a reference to the previous block, creating a chronological chain. This chain of blocks forms the blockchain. The transactions within a block are verified by multiple participants in the network, known as "miners" in the case of cryptocurrencies, who use computational power to solve complex mathematical puzzles.

Once a block is verified, it is added to the blockchain, and the information becomes permanent and tamper-proof. This distributed nature of blockchain ensures that no single entity can control or manipulate the data. Anyone with access to the blockchain can independently verify the integrity of transactions, enhancing transparency and trust within the network.

Moreover, blockchain's decentralized nature makes it resilient to attacks and failures. Since the data is distributed across multiple computers, it is not reliant on a single point of failure. This feature enhances the security and reliability of the blockchain network.

In summary, cryptography is the art and science of securing communication, while blockchain is a decentralized and transparent digital ledger. By combining the two, blockchain technology ensures the security and integrity of transactions, enabling trust and facilitating various applications beyond cryptocurrencies.

Imagine you want to send money to a friend across the globe without going through banks and paying hefty fees. Cryptocurrencies enable you to do just that, allowing you to transfer funds directly, with reduced costs and increased speed. You will witness the power of blockchain technology as you explore the transaction history, which remains accessible to everyone while protecting the privacy of individual users.

Financial revolution in which cryptocurrencies emerge is the catalyst for a new era of financial freedom. From decentralized networks blossoming like vibrant ecosystems to cryptography acting as an impenetrable fortress guarding digital assets, you will gain a profound appreciation for the transformative potential of cryptocurrencies.

So, fasten your seatbelts and get ready to dive into the thrilling realm of cryptocurrencies, where innovation and disruption converge to shape the future of finance.

Chapter 2: Introduction To Blockchain Technology

Welcome to the captivating realm of blockchain technology, where innovation and trust intertwine to shape the future of various industries. In this unit, we will embark on a journey to understand the intricacies of blockchain, exploring its components, consensus mechanisms, different types of blockchain, the power of smart contracts, and the vital considerations of privacy and security.

1. Understanding blockchain and its components:

Imagine a grand woven textile, meticulously woven together from numerous threads of information. That woven textile is the blockchain, a decentralized and transparent digital ledger that records transactions across a network of computers. Each transaction is grouped into a block, forming a chain of interconnected blocks that create an immutable record.

To illustrate this, let's step into the bustling world of real estate. Picture a property transaction recorded on a blockchain. Every detail, from the buyer's and seller's identities to the property's history, is etched into a block. Once verified, the block is added to the chain, forever preserving the transaction's authenticity.

2. Consensus mechanisms: Proof of Work, Proof of Stake, etc.:

In the blockchain realm, consensus is the glue that binds the network together, ensuring agreement on the validity of transactions. Consensus mechanisms, like Proof of Work (PoW) and Proof of Stake (PoS), play a crucial role in achieving this harmony.

Consensus mechanism is a fundamental concept in blockchain technology that enables agreement among participants in a decentralized network on the validity and order of transactions. It ensures that all nodes in the network come to a consensus about the state of the blockchain without the need for a central authority.

To understand consensus mechanisms better, let's explore relatable examples:

(i). Proof of Work (PoW):

Imagine a group of puzzle enthusiasts competing to solve a challenging puzzle. In PoW, participants, called miners, use computational power to solve complex mathematical puzzles. The first miner to find a solution announces it to the network. The other participants then verify the solution, and once consensus is reached, the block is added to the blockchain, and the miner is rewarded. This mechanism is resource-intensive but provides a high level of security, as altering the blockchain would require immense computational power.

Let's envision a bustling marketplace where sellers vie for the attention of buyers. In the realm of PoW, sellers showcase their computational power by solving complex mathematical puzzles. The first to solve it gains the right to validate the block of transactions.

(ii). Proof of Stake (PoS):

Let's envision a scenario where a group of individuals with varying amounts of cryptocurrency tokens participates in a decision-making process. In PoS, participants "stake" their tokens by locking them up as collateral. The probability of being chosen to validate a block and receive rewards is proportional to the number of tokens staked. This mechanism promotes energy efficiency compared to PoW and reduces the dominance of participants with excessive computational power.

In PoS, on the other hand, sellers stake their ownership of cryptocurrency, like tokens, and the probability of validating a block is determined by the amount they hold.

(iii). Delegated Proof of Stake (DPoS):

Picture a board of directors responsible for decision-making in a company. In DPoS, token holders vote to elect a limited number of delegates who are responsible for validating transactions and adding blocks to the blockchain. These delegates take turns to perform the validation, ensuring efficiency and scalability in the network. DPoS combines the benefits of decentralization with faster transaction processing times.

(iv). Practical Byzantine Fault Tolerance (PBFT):

Imagine a group of friends trying to reach a consensus on where to go for dinner. Each person proposes their choice, and the group votes. PBFT is a consensus mechanism that works similarly. In a decentralized network, a designated leader (or a rotating set of leaders) proposes a block of transactions, and other nodes in the network vote on its validity. Consensus is reached when a threshold of votes is achieved, and the block is added to the blockchain.

These examples illustrate how consensus mechanisms function in blockchain networks. Each mechanism balances factors such as security, decentralization, scalability, and energy efficiency in different ways. By achieving consensus, blockchain networks ensure the integrity and immutability of the distributed ledger, making it trustworthy and resistant to tampering or fraud.

3. Types of blockchain: public, private, and consortium:

Blockchain offers various shades to cater to diverse needs. There are public blockchains, like Bitcoin and Ethereum, open to all participants. In contrast, private blockchains restrict access to a select few entities. Imagine a private island accessible only to a trusted circle of individuals. Consortium blockchains strike a balance, forming a group of pre-selected participants who jointly maintain and govern the blockchain. Picture a table where stakeholders from different industries gather, forging alliances to develop a blockchain ecosystem that serves their collective interests.

4. Smart contracts and their applications:

Smart contracts are the crown jewels of blockchain, enabling self-executing agreements with predefined conditions. Imagine a digital contract infused with magical properties. When the conditions encoded within the contract are met, it springs to life, autonomously executing the agreed-upon actions.

Let's explore a supply chain scenario where smart contracts revolutionize transparency and efficiency. When a product changes hands, the smart contract triggers automatic updates across the blockchain, ensuring real-time visibility into the product's journey, reducing fraud and ensuring adherence to quality standards.

Here are more examples of smart contracts and their potential applications:

(i). Supply Chain Management: Smart contracts can streamline and automate supply chain processes. For instance, a smart contract can be programmed to trigger automatic payments to suppliers when certain conditions are met, such as successful delivery or quality verification of goods. This eliminates the need for intermediaries, reduces disputes, and enhances transparency throughout the supply chain.

(ii). Insurance Claims: Smart contracts can revolutionize the insurance industry by automating claims processing. When an insured event occurs, such as a car accident, the smart contract can automatically assess the validity of the claim based on predefined conditions. If the conditions are met, the contract can initiate the payout to the policyholder, eliminating the need for manual claim processing and reducing fraud.

(iii). Real Estate Transactions: Buying or selling property involves complex processes and intermediaries. Smart contracts can simplify and expedite these transactions. The contract can be programmed to automatically transfer ownership rights to the buyer once the payment is received, eliminating the need for intermediaries such as lawyers and title companies. It also ensures transparency in the transaction history and simplifies the transfer of funds.

(iv). Decentralized Finance (DeFi): Smart contracts are at the core of DeFi applications, which aim to provide traditional financial services, such as lending, borrowing, and trading, using blockchain technology. For example, a smart contract can facilitate a peer-to-peer lending platform where borrowers can access loans directly from lenders, without the need for traditional financial institutions. The contract automates loan terms, interest rates, and repayment schedules, ensuring secure and transparent transactions.

(v). Intellectual Property Rights: Smart contracts can streamline the management and licensing of intellectual property (IP) rights. For instance, artists can use smart contracts to automatically enforce copyright protection and receive royalties whenever their digital artwork is sold or used. The contracts can define the terms, conditions, and payment structure, ensuring fair compensation for creators and eliminating the need for intermediaries.

(iv). Voting Systems: Smart contracts can enhance the transparency and security of voting systems. By recording votes on a blockchain, the process becomes tamper-proof and verifiable. Smart contracts can ensure that only eligible voters can participate, prevent double voting, and automatically tally the results accurately. This can lead to more secure and trustworthy elections.

These examples showcase the versatility of smart contracts in various industries and highlight their potential to automate processes, reduce intermediaries, increase efficiency, and enhance transparency and trust.

As blockchain technology continues to evolve, smart contracts are poised to revolutionize traditional systems and open up new possibilities for automation and decentralized applications.

5. Privacy and security considerations in blockchain:

As we journey deeper into the blockchain realm, we encounter the twin pillars of privacy and security. Blockchain upholds the principles of transparency and immutability while safeguarding sensitive information.

Imagine a secure vault hidden within the blockchain, where personal data resides. The vault protects privacy by encrypting the data, allowing only authorized parties with cryptographic keys to access it. Furthermore, blockchain's decentralized nature mitigates the risk of single points of failure, making it resilient against attacks and ensuring the integrity of stored data.

In conclusion, we have painted a vivid picture of blockchain technology. From the intricate woven textile of interconnected blocks to magical contracts and secure vaults, the power of blockchain unfolds, revolutionizing industries and redefining trust in the digital age. As we navigate the complexities of consensus mechanisms, different types of blockchain, smart contracts, and privacy and security considerations, we unlock the potential of blockchain and its limitless applications.

Chapter 3: Bitcoin: The First Cryptocurrency

Welcome to the world of Bitcoin, a digital currency that has revolutionized the financial landscape. In this unit, we will embark on an adventure to explore the origins of Bitcoin, delve into the captivating process of Bitcoin mining and transaction verification, understand the various Bitcoin wallet options for storing this digital gold, examine its potential as an investment with its risks and rewards, and unravel the regulatory and legal challenges that surround this groundbreaking cryptocurrency.

1. Overview of Bitcoin and its origins:

Imagine a mysterious figure, known as Satoshi Nakamoto, whose true identity remains hidden like a hidden treasure. It was in 2009 when Nakamoto unveiled Bitcoin to the world, introducing a decentralized digital currency that would disrupt the traditional financial system. Bitcoin, often referred to as digital gold, is built on a foundation of blockchain technology, ensuring security, transparency, and immutability.

Let's imagine a bustling digital marketplace where merchants and buyers interact, like a vibrant bazaar of the internet. Bitcoin emerges as the universal currency, transcending borders and eliminating intermediaries. Its scarcity, with a limited supply of 21 million coins, grants it a unique value proposition, akin to a precious gem that becomes increasingly rare as time passes.

2. Bitcoin mining and transaction verification:

Let's venture into the vast Bitcoin mines, where miners don their virtual helmets and pickaxes, striving to unearth new Bitcoin treasures. Bitcoin mining involves solving complex mathematical puzzles using computational power. Miners compete to be the first to find the solution, validating transactions and adding them to the blockchain. This process ensures the security and integrity of the Bitcoin network, akin to miners sifting through layers of rock to extract valuable gems.

In our story, each transaction is like a shimmering gemstone, waiting to be verified and added to the blockchain. Miners, like diligent gemologists, meticulously examine each transaction, ensuring its authenticity and preventing fraud. Once approved, the transaction becomes a part of the immutable ledger, sparkling in the vast sea of digital gems.

Bitcoin Mining Process:

Bitcoin mining involves the process of validating and adding new transactions to the blockchain. Miners compete to solve complex mathematical puzzles, and the first miner to find the solution earns the right to add a new block of transactions to the blockchain, along with a reward in the form of newly minted Bitcoins.

Imagine a bustling mining farm, filled with rows of powerful computers running day and night, akin to an industrial-scale operation. These computers, known as mining rigs, consist of specialized hardware designed to perform the necessary computations required for mining. Miners harness their computational power to generate hash functions, seeking a specific pattern that satisfies the network's difficulty requirements.

As an analogy, consider a massive treasure hunt with thousands of participants searching for a hidden key to unlock a vault. Each miner's mining rig represents their dedicated effort to find that elusive key. The more computational power a miner possesses, the higher their chances of being the first to solve the puzzle and earn the mining reward.

Energy Consumption of Mining Farms:

Bitcoin mining farms consume a significant amount of energy due to the computational power required to mine Bitcoins. The energy consumption is primarily attributed to the high-performance hardware and the continuous operation of mining rigs.

To put the energy consumption in perspective, imagine a mining farm consuming energy equivalent to a small town or even a country. The energy usage can be substantial, comparable to the energy consumed by industries or large-scale data centers. This is due to the energy-intensive nature of the mining process, which requires miners to continuously run their rigs to compete for rewards.

Location of Mining Farms:

Bitcoin mining farms are located in various regions around the world, with certain factors influencing their geographical distribution. One critical factor is the availability and cost of electricity. Mining farms tend to be situated in areas with abundant and relatively inexpensive electricity sources, as it directly impacts the profitability of mining operations.

For example, regions with access to cheap hydroelectric power, such as China's Sichuan province, have attracted a significant number of mining farms. Other locations with favorable conditions, such as Iceland and Scandinavia, leverage renewable energy sources like geothermal and hydroelectric power.

Additionally, mining farms can be found in countries with favorable regulatory environments and political stability, as these factors contribute to a conducive operating environment for miners.

It's important to note that the location of mining farms can shift over time as mining economics and regulations evolve. Miners often seek out regions where they can maximize their operational efficiency while minimizing energy costs.

Overall, the energy consumption of mining farms and their distribution across different regions underscores the significant impact of Bitcoin mining on global energy consumption. The quest to balance energy efficiency and sustainability within the mining industry remains an ongoing endeavor, with efforts being made to explore renewable energy sources and improve the energy efficiency of mining hardware.

3. Bitcoin wallets and storage options:

As the value of Bitcoin increases, individuals seek secure storage solutions to safeguard their digital fortune. Picture a vault hidden within the virtual realm, accessible only through encrypted keys. Bitcoin wallets serve as these virtual vaults, offering various options for storing and accessing Bitcoin securely.

Imagine a traveler carrying a digital wallet on their smartphone, akin to a magic pouch that holds their precious gems. This mobile wallet provides convenience and accessibility, enabling them to use Bitcoin for transactions on the go. Alternatively, envision a hardware wallet, like an impregnable fortress guarding the gems, disconnected from the internet to ensure maximum security. Each wallet option offers a unique combination of convenience and protection, empowering users to safeguard their digital wealth.

The concepts of custodian and non-custodian Bitcoin wallets, highlighting their characteristics and how they differ in terms of control and security.

(i). Custodian Bitcoin Wallets:

Custodian wallets, also known as hosted wallets, are Bitcoin wallets where a third-party entity, such as a cryptocurrency exchange or a financial institution, holds and manages the private keys on behalf of the user. When using a custodian wallet, the user entrusts the custody and security of their Bitcoin to the custodian service provider.

Imagine a safe deposit box at a bank. In a custodian Bitcoin wallet, the third-party custodian acts as the "bank" that securely stores and manages the private keys associated with the user's Bitcoin. The user accesses their Bitcoin holdings through the custodian's platform or interface, typically through a username and password.

Custodian wallets offer convenience and ease of use, as the custodian handles the technical complexities of managing private keys and ensuring security. They are often used by individuals who prefer a simpler user experience or who may not have the technical expertise to handle their own private keys.

However, using a custodian wallet means placing trust in the custodian to safeguard the Bitcoin. The custodian has control over the private keys, which introduces a level of counterparty risk. If the custodian experiences a security breach or goes out of business, there is a risk of potential loss or restricted access to the Bitcoin held in the custodian wallet.

(ii). Non-Custodian Bitcoin Wallets:

Non-custodian wallets, also known as self-custody or self-hosted wallets, provide users with full control over their private keys. These wallets allow individuals to manage their Bitcoin holdings independently, without relying on a third-party custodian. Non-custodian wallets can take various forms, including software wallets, hardware wallets, or even paper wallets.

Imagine a personal safe at home. In a non-custodian Bitcoin wallet, the user retains sole ownership and control of the private keys, which are stored securely on their own device or in physical form. The user is responsible for protecting and safeguarding their private keys from unauthorized access or loss.

Non-custodian wallets prioritize user control and security. By holding the private keys, individuals have full autonomy over their Bitcoin transactions and can maintain privacy. The use of non-custodian wallets aligns with the decentralized nature of cryptocurrencies, as users are not reliant on any central authority.

However, with this increased control comes added responsibility. Users must take precautions to protect their private keys from theft, loss, or damage. Without the assistance of a custodian, there is no recourse if the private keys are lost or stolen. Therefore, individuals using non-custodian wallets must prioritize security measures such as strong passwords, encryption, and regular backups.

In summary, custodian Bitcoin wallets offer convenience but require trust in a third-party custodian, while non-custodian wallets provide users with full control over their private keys but require greater personal responsibility for security. The choice between custodian and non-custodian wallets depends on individual preferences, technical expertise, and the desired level of control and security over Bitcoin holdings.

4. Bitcoin as an investment: risks and rewards:

The allure of Bitcoin as an investment has captivated many, akin to the rush of a treasure hunt. Its price volatility offers both opportunities and risks. Just as a brave adventurer sets sail in search of hidden treasures, Bitcoin investors navigate the unpredictable waves of the market.

Picture an investor gazing at the price chart, observing the rise and fall of Bitcoin like a roller coaster ride. With each twist and turn, fortunes are made and lost. The potential rewards are captivating, as early investors have witnessed meteoric rises in Bitcoin's value. However, the risks are ever-present, as market fluctuations and regulatory developments can cause sharp downturns. Investors must navigate this treacherous landscape with caution and strategic decision-making.

Bitcoin's value has experienced significant growth over time, accompanied by notable price fluctuations. Since its inception in 2009, Bitcoin has evolved from a virtually worthless asset to a highly valued cryptocurrency. Let's explore its value growth and the nature of price fluctuations.

1. Early Years and Price Discovery:

In its early years, Bitcoin had minimal adoption and trading volume, resulting in extremely low prices. In 2010, the first known commercial transaction using Bitcoin took place when two pizzas were purchased for 10,000 BTC, highlighting the nascent and experimental nature of the cryptocurrency.

Bitcoin's value gradually started to appreciate as more people became aware of its potential. By mid-2011, its price reached around $1, reflecting a significant milestone in Bitcoin's value discovery process. However, during this period, price volatility was relatively high due to the small market size and limited liquidity.

2. Breakthrough Moments and Price Surges:

Bitcoin's value experienced notable breakthrough moments that propelled it to new heights. In 2013, Bitcoin captured the attention of the mainstream media and investors as its price surged from around $13 to over $200. This price increase was driven by increased public awareness, growing acceptance, and the emergence of cryptocurrency exchanges.

Another significant price surge occurred in late 2013 when Bitcoin reached an all-time high of nearly $1,200. However, this was followed by a sharp correction, leading to a prolonged bear market period.

3. Bull Markets and All-Time Highs:

Bitcoin's price history is punctuated by cycles of bull markets and bear markets. Bull markets are characterized by significant price appreciation, often driven by increased institutional adoption, regulatory developments, and market speculation. These periods have seen Bitcoin reach new all-time highs.

One of the most remarkable bull markets occurred in late 2017 and early 2018. Bitcoin's price skyrocketed from around $1,000 at the beginning of 2017 to an all-time high of nearly $20,000 in December 2017. However, this was followed by a severe bear market, with prices plummeting to around $3,000 by the end of 2018.

Bitcoin entered a new bull market phase in 2020, driven by increased institutional interest, macroeconomic uncertainty, and the mainstream adoption of cryptocurrencies. In early 2021, Bitcoin reached new all-time highs, surpassing $60,000, reflecting the growing acceptance and recognition of its value.

4. Price Volatility and Market Fluctuations:

Bitcoin's price volatility has been a characteristic feature throughout its history. Price fluctuations of several percentage points within a single day are not uncommon. Bitcoin's volatility is influenced by various factors, including market sentiment, regulatory announcements, macroeconomic events, and technological advancements.

The decentralized and speculative nature of the cryptocurrency market can lead to sudden price movements. While Bitcoin has witnessed substantial price increases, it has also experienced sharp corrections and extended bear market periods.

It's important to note that Bitcoin's value growth and price fluctuations are inherent to the cryptocurrency's nature. The market remains highly speculative, and price movements can be influenced by a wide range of factors. Investors and participants should be aware of the risks associated with Bitcoin's volatility and exercise caution when engaging in trading or investment activities.

5. Regulatory and legal challenges surrounding Bitcoin:

In our story, regulatory and legal challenges lurk like sea monsters in the vast ocean of Bitcoin. Governments and regulatory bodies strive to establish frameworks and guidelines to address concerns such as money laundering, tax evasion, and consumer protection.

Imagine a global summit where regulators from different nations convene, seeking to tame the wild waves of Bitcoin. They grapple with questions of jurisdiction, defining legal status, and formulating policies to strike a delicate balance between innovation and regulation. The path towards regulatory clarity is akin to charting uncharted territories, requiring collaboration and adaptability to ensure a sustainable and secure ecosystem for Bitcoin and its users.

As our Bitcoin adventure concludes, we have explored the origins and transformative potential of this digital currency. From the thrilling process of mining and transaction verification to the importance of secure Bitcoin wallets, the risks and rewards of investment, and the regulatory challenges, we have unveiled the multifaceted nature of

Bitcoin. Its journey continues, shaped by technology, market dynamics, and the evolving landscape of regulation.

Chapter 4: Navigating the World of Cryptocurrencies

In this chapter, we delve into the fascinating realm of cryptocurrencies, exploring various aspects that every crypto enthusiast should be familiar with. From altcoins to cryptocurrency wallets, from investing to regulation, we will traverse through the diverse landscape of this digital revolution.

1. Altcoins and Examples:

Altcoins, short for alternative coins, refer to any cryptocurrency other than Bitcoin, which was the first and most well-known crypto. The crypto market is now teeming with a plethora of altcoins, each with its unique features and use cases. Examples of popular altcoins include Ethereum, which is renowned for its smart contract capabilities, Ripple (XRP) used for cross-border payments, and Litecoin, known for its faster transaction times. As the crypto world continues to evolve, new altcoins emerge, adding depth and diversity to the digital currency ecosystem.

2. Types of Cryptocurrency Exchanges: Centralized, Decentralized, Peer-to-Peer:

Cryptocurrency exchanges play a crucial role in enabling the buying, selling, and trading of cryptocurrencies. There are three main types of exchanges:

- Centralized Exchanges: These are traditional platforms where a centralized authority manages and controls the exchange. Users deposit their cryptocurrencies into the exchange's wallet and trade through the platform. Examples of centralized exchanges include Binance and Coinbase.

- Decentralized Exchanges (DEX): DEX operates without a central authority and instead relies on smart contracts to facilitate peer-to-peer trading. This decentralized nature provides users with greater control over their funds and reduces the risk of hacking. Uniswap and PancakeSwap are examples of popular DEX platforms.

- Peer-to-Peer (P2P) Exchanges: In P2P exchanges, users directly interact with each other to trade cryptocurrencies, often facilitated through an escrow system. P2P exchanges enable users to trade with more privacy and avoid centralized intermediaries. LocalBitcoins and Paxful are well-known P2P platforms.

3. Cryptocurrency Wallets and Security:

Cryptocurrency wallets are essential tools that enable users to store, send, and receive their digital assets securely. There are two main types of wallets:

- Hardware Wallets: These are physical devices (e.g., Ledger and Trezor) that store private keys offline, providing a high level of security and protection against hacking.

- Software Wallets: Software wallets come in various forms, including desktop, mobile, and web-based wallets. While convenient for regular transactions, they can be more susceptible to online threats. Examples include Exodus (desktop), Trust Wallet (mobile), and MetaMask (web-based).

To ensure the utmost security, practicing good wallet hygiene, such as using strong passwords, enabling two-factor authentication, and keeping backup copies of wallet recovery phrases in a safe place is vital.

4. Cryptocurrency Investing and Trading:

Cryptocurrency investing and trading offer opportunities for potential growth and profits. Investors can buy and hold cryptocurrencies for the long term, hoping that their value will increase over time. On the other hand, traders engage in short-term buying and selling, aiming to profit from price fluctuations.

However, it is essential to recognize that the crypto market can be highly volatile and speculative. Therefore, prudent risk management and thorough research are crucial for successful investing and trading. Understanding market trends, analyzing charts, and staying informed about the latest developments are essential components of a well-informed crypto strategy.

5. Regulation and Compliance:

As cryptocurrencies gain popularity, governments and regulatory bodies worldwide have begun to develop guidelines and regulations to oversee the crypto industry. The regulatory landscape varies from country to country, with some embracing cryptocurrencies and blockchain technology while others are more cautious.

Cryptocurrency users and businesses must adhere to the relevant laws and regulations in their jurisdictions to ensure compliance and avoid legal issues. Factors such as taxation, anti-money laundering (AML) measures, and Know Your Customer (KYC) policies may apply, depending on the region.

Conclusion:

Navigating the world of cryptocurrencies requires a comprehensive understanding of altcoins, various types of exchanges, wallet security, investment strategies, and compliance with regulations. As this digital revolution continues to unfold, staying informed and adopting best practices will empower crypto enthusiasts to participate responsibly and reap the potential benefits of this dynamic and transformative space.

Part II: Introduction to Pi Network

Chapter 5: Pi Mining App

After downloading the Pi Mining App from Google Play Store or App Store, you embark on a journey that requires attention to detail and remember to fill in the invitation code of the pioneer who invited you. If you don't have any invitation code use "oriungu". Like a brave adventurer, you fill in the necessary details, ensuring that your name on the Identity document matches exactly, which will be a crucial to pass KYC.

As you explore the Pi Mining App, you are greeted with a wealth of features that empower you to take charge of your mining journey. At the top:

(i). Your total mined Pi shines brightly, adorned with bonuses from your referral team and security team, like sparkling gems in your treasure trove.

On the right side of the app. You find an array of tools that unlock the potential of Pi.

(ii). At the top choose your preferred language, like selecting the perfect wand for your magical spells.

(iii). Following is Chat, engage with different community groups and discussions through the Chat feature, immersing yourself in the heart of the Pi Network community.

(iv). Next is Security, embrace the spirit of security by forming your own team of guardians. Add four members to your security team to maintain the network's safety, ensuring that your status stands tall at 100%

(v). Your referral team icon stands down from the security, displaying the total number of pioneers who have joined through your link, including those actively mining

(iv). The Lightning button, a mystical symbol of persistence, holds a potent secret. Every 24 hours, you click it with unwavering dedication, renewing your mining session and channeling your commitment to the Pi Network's success

Turn your attention to the left side of the app, where a treasure trove of applications awaits. When you click navigating bar at the top a list of features shows up:

1. The Home page greets you where the Core Team's regularly post updates, and in its bottom there is button from where you can invite others to join the Pi Network, expanding the community of pioneers.

2. Mainnet the second feature, venture further into the Mainnet page , where the true value of Pi begins to unfold. Unverified balance, transferable balance, and transferred Pi to Mainnet represent the blossoming fruits of your mining efforts. Here, you find the Mainnet checklist, a roadmap to unlocking the full potential of your mined Pi Configure Lockup Setting is a magical feature that regulates the Pi supply in the ecosystem, ensuring its balance and harmony. You have the power to notify your team to complete KYC and migrate, like a herald calling for the gathering of allies.

3. Browser: Intrigued by the world of applications, you can access the Browser from the mining app, leading you to a realm of diverse utilities that we will explore in greater detail in future chapters.

4. Utilities: The only utility on the mining app is the chat app, which we looked at on the home page.

5. Transfer: This was mostly crucial during the early stages, during the testnet period when in-app Pi transfer was enabled. As the network has developed, this function might not be very important.

6. Mine Pi: As you delve into Mine Pi, a treasure trove of information awaits. Your mining activity is laid bare, displaying the remaining time

for each session, your hourly mining rate, and the various bonuses and rewards that enrich your journey.

7. Referral Team: With your referral team at your side, you can navigate their details, urging inactive members to join the quest. You have opportunity to start your team chat group a place for connection and collaboration among your referrals.

8. Node: Here, those interested in running nodes on their computers can start. Briefly, in the context of blockchain technology, a node refers to any device or computer that participates in maintaining and validating the network. Each node contains a copy of the entire blockchain's transaction history and follows the rules of the consensus mechanism to validate and confirm transactions. Nodes work together to ensure the security, transparency, and decentralization of the blockchain network by reaching a consensus on the validity of transactions and new blocks. They play a crucial role in maintaining the integrity of the blockchain and supporting the distributed nature of the system.

9. Frequently Asked Questions. FAQS

10. White Paper: This is the comprehensive and authoritative document that outlines the vision, objectives, technical details, and implementation plans of a Pi Network project, technology, or initiative. It serves as a foundational blueprint, providing users with in-depth information about the project's purpose, mechanics, token economics, and roadmap.

11. Core Team: This page contains profile details of the project founders.

12. Profile: This page contains the pioneer's details.

13. Core Team Social Media Handles: These are the official social media platforms. Pioneers should only trust information communicated through these platforms. Don't fall prey to online scammers impersonating themselves as Core team representatives.

Chapter 6: Pi Network History

Once upon a digital horizon, where dreams converged with innovation, a group of visionaries stepped into the realm of endless possibilities. They dared to dream of a decentralized world, where the power of currency lay not in the hands of a few, but in the hearts of many. And so, the story of Pi Network began, a tale woven with the threads of hope and the ingenuity of pioneers.

In the digital realm of boundless imagination, the Pi Network was ignited by a triumvirate of pioneers: Dr. Nicolas Kokkalis, Dr. Chengdiao Fan, and Vincent McPhillip.

In the virtual valley of Stanford, where knowledge and brilliance flowed like a river, the founders gathered, much like stars forming constellations in the night sky. Each one, a beacon of talent, brought their unique expertise to the table, aligning their cosmic energies for a greater purpose.

Amidst their virtual symposiums and virtual coffee breaks, they hatched a grand plan, an ambitious venture to redefine the landscape of cryptocurrency. They aimed to dismantle the barriers that confined mining to the domain of a privileged few, making it accessible to every soul with a mobile device.

Like alchemists of old, they concocted a formula that defied convention - "Proof-of-Trust." No longer would the measure of wealth be brute computational strength, but rather, the trust individuals placed in one another. With this revelation, they sowed the seeds of a new era, where trust and unity were the pillars supporting the Pi Network.

As the dawn of Pi Network approached, they carved a path with sheer dedication and resolve, weathering storms of skepticism and doubt. Like pioneers forging trails through uncharted territories, they paved the way for an ecosystem of empowerment, where users' voices mattered and contributions were valued.

Dr. Nicolas Kokkalis

Dr. Nicolas Kokkalis, a luminary from the halls of Stanford, possessed a vision that extended beyond the horizon of conventional thought. With his brilliant mind and passion for innovation, he laid the foundation for the Pi Network's revolutionary consensus mechanism.

Dr. Nicolas Kokkalis, a distinguished figure in the academic realm, emerged from the hallowed halls of Stanford University, armed with a profound intellect and an insatiable curiosity. Throughout his academic journey, he demonstrated an exceptional grasp of complex concepts, earning him the reputation of a luminary in various fields of study.

With an unwavering commitment to pushing the boundaries of knowledge, Dr. Kokkalis delved into the intricate world of blockchain and cryptocurrencies. While many saw these emerging technologies as mere novelties, he envisioned their potential to reshape the very fabric of our financial systems.

Driven by an innate desire to challenge the status quo, Dr. Kokkalis became deeply engrossed in understanding the limitations of existing consensus mechanisms, particularly the resource-intensive and energy-guzzling proof-of-work used by many prominent cryptocurrencies.

It was during this intellectual exploration that the seeds of the Pi Network's revolutionary consensus mechanism were sown. Dr. Kokkalis conceived an ingenious approach that would not only ensure network security but also empower everyday users to participate in the mining process without the need for specialized hardware.

Drawing inspiration from the concept of trust and social networks, he developed the "Proof-of-Trust" consensus mechanism. In this novel approach, individuals mine Pi by attesting to their trust in the network daily. This innovative system harnessed the power of human relationships and user interactions, allowing Pi Network to foster a sense of community and cooperation.

With an understanding that accessibility was the key to mass adoption, Dr. Kokkalis and the Pi Network team designed the mobile mining feature, enabling anyone with a smartphone to contribute to the network's growth. This approach was a paradigm shift, democratizing mining and challenging the traditional notion that cryptocurrency mining was the preserve of a select few with expensive mining rigs.

The brilliance of Dr. Kokkalis' vision lay not only in the technical aspects of the consensus mechanism but also in the overarching philosophy of empowerment and inclusion. The Pi Network became a beacon of hope for those who had previously been excluded from the world of cryptocurrencies, providing them with an opportunity to participate and be part of something greater.

As the Pi Network gained momentum, Dr. Kokkalis' passion for innovation and tireless dedication to the project became evident to the entire community. His guidance and leadership acted as a driving force, inspiring others to share in his vision and join the mission to redefine the landscape of cryptocurrency.

In the grand tapestry of the Pi Network's history, Dr. Nicolas Kokkalis stood as a foundational pillar, a visionary who dared to dream beyond the limits of conventional thought. His brilliant mind and passion for innovation laid the groundwork for the Pi Network's ascent, forever etching his name in the annals of technological progress and human ingenuity.

Dr. Chengdiao Fan

At his side stood Dr. Chengdiao Fan, a force of nature in the world of computer science. Her expertise in distributed systems for social interaction and blockchain technologies breathed life into the Pi Network's vision, allowing it to transcend boundaries.

Dr. Chengdiao Fan, a formidable force in the realm of computer science, emerged as a key figure at the side of Dr. Nicolas Kokkalis during the inception of the Pi Network. With a brilliant mind and a deep understanding of distributed systems and social interactions, she brought invaluable expertise to the table, fortifying the Pi Network's vision with technical prowess.

Drawing upon a wealth of experience and knowledge in the intricacies of distributed systems, Dr. Fan recognized the potential of blockchain technology to revolutionize not only the financial sector but also social interactions and community dynamics. She understood that the true power of blockchain lay not solely in financial transactions but in its capacity to foster trust and cooperation within networks of individuals.

In the tapestry of the Pi Network's vision, Dr. Fan played a pivotal role in crafting the architecture that underpinned the entire ecosystem. The innovative "Proof-of-Trust" consensus mechanism, conceived by Dr. Nicolas Kokkalis, found its lifeblood through Dr. Fan's expertise in distributed systems. She engineered the technical framework that enabled users to seamlessly attest to their trust in the network daily, forming the foundation of the Pi Network's unique approach to mining.

As the Pi Network aspired to transcend boundaries and unite a global community, Dr. Fan's mastery of social interactions within distributed systems became increasingly crucial. She recognized that building a strong and interconnected community was vital to the success of the project. By integrating social elements into the Pi Network's design, she fostered an environment where users could forge meaningful connections, share experiences, and collaborate towards a shared vision.

With every line of code she crafted, Dr. Fan breathed life into the Pi Network's grand vision, aligning its technical infrastructure with its overarching philosophy of empowerment and inclusion. Her contributions paved the way for a cryptocurrency ecosystem that celebrated not only financial transactions but also the human relationships that formed its backbone.

The fusion of Dr. Fan's expertise in distributed systems and blockchain technologies became a testament to the power of technology in reshaping the way we interact, transact, and collaborate.

Beyond her technical brilliance, Dr. Fan's dedication to the project was unwavering. Like a force of nature, she channeled her energy into propelling the Pi Network forward, responding to challenges with resilience and innovation. Her presence at Dr. Kokkalis' side provided the project with a solid technical anchor, ensuring that the Pi Network's vision remained grounded in practicality and feasibility.

Vincent McPhillip

Completing the trinity was Vincent McPhillip, a visionary entrepreneur with a keen eye for the potential of blockchain. Drawing upon his experiences in the tech world, he charted the course for the Pi Network's user-centric journey.

Completing the trinity of founders was Vincent McPhillip, an extraordinary visionary entrepreneur who possessed a profound understanding of the transformative potential of blockchain technology. With a keen eye for recognizing opportunities and trends in the tech world, he embarked on a mission to chart a user-centric journey for the Pi Network.

Drawing upon his diverse experiences in the technology industry, Vincent McPhillip brought a unique perspective to the Pi Network's founding team. His entrepreneurial spirit and strategic acumen became instrumental in shaping the project's direction and growth trajectory.

As a visionary, Vincent saw beyond the immediate applications of blockchain and envisioned a future where this transformative technology could empower individuals across the globe. His passion for blockchain's decentralizing ethos fueled his determination to create a cryptocurrency that would be accessible to all, transcending geographical and socioeconomic barriers.

With a finger on the pulse of the tech landscape, Vincent understood that user adoption and engagement were critical factors in the success of any digital endeavor. Emphasizing a user-centric approach, he collaborated with his fellow founders to design the Pi Network's ecosystem with accessibility and inclusivity in mind.

Through Vincent's guidance, the Pi Network cultivated an environment that encouraged participation and community-building. The invitation-based system during the network's early stages fostered a sense of belonging, encouraging users to actively invite and engage with others. This organic growth strategy created a tightly-knit community, united by a shared passion for the Pi Network's mission.

Vincent's strategic vision extended beyond the confines of early adoption, foreseeing the potential for mass-scale integration of the Pi Network into everyday life. He sought to create a platform that could seamlessly integrate into users' daily routines, making the concept of cryptocurrency mining as effortless as sending a message on a smartphone.

His approach also prioritized trust and transparency, instilling confidence in the Pi Network's community. The network's emphasis on secure and ethical practices became a cornerstone of its reputation, inspiring users to entrust their daily interactions and attestations with conviction.

As the Pi Network evolved, so did Vincent's role as a guiding force. He championed the project's growth, leading strategic initiatives to ensure the network's stability and scalability. With each milestone, he remained at the forefront, advocating for a harmonious balance between innovation and user welfare.

In the epic tale of the Pi Network's history, Vincent McPhillip emerged as a beacon of vision and entrepreneurship. His keen eye for the potential of blockchain, combined with a user-centric approach, charted the course for the Pi Network's global journey. Vincent's legacy became etched in the project's DNA, fueling its drive to empower individuals worldwide and realize the founders' collective dream of creating a truly accessible and inclusive cryptocurrency ecosystem.

Pi Day: 14th March 2019

On that fateful day, the 14th of March 2019, the Pi Network was officially born. Like cosmic stardust, the first block was mined, and from that moment, the journey to redefine cryptocurrency had begun.

Through storms and sunshine, the trio persisted with unwavering dedication. They shepherded the Pi Network through its early stages, carefully nurturing it like a sapling in the digital wilderness.

As word of Pi Network spread, a global constellation of users assembled. They hailed from all corners of the world, united by the dream of a decentralized and inclusive future. Their trust in the founders and the network formed the bedrock upon which the Pi Network thrived.

In the years that followed, the Pi Network community flourished like a garden in full bloom. Through ongoing innovation, the founders ensured that the Pi Network's roots ran deep, providing a stable and fertile ground for its growth.

And so, the legacy of Dr. Nicolas Kokkalis, Dr. Chengdiao Fan, and Vincent McPhillip became inscribed in the virtual annals of history. They had kindled a fire that would illuminate the path towards a new era of cryptocurrency, forever remembered as the pioneers of the Pi Network.

Chapter 7: Embracing the PIONEER'S Spirit

Pi Requires Patience, Dedication, and Hard Work, Not a Shortcut to Quick and Easy Money

In the ethereal world of cryptocurrencies, the allure of quick, easy, and free money often casts a spell on those seeking a path to instant riches. However, as pioneers of the Pi Network, we must embrace the true essence of the PIONEER spirit and understand that Pi is not a magical fountain of overnight wealth. Instead, it represents a journey of community, dedication, and patience. Let use Acronym PIONEER to describe this Spirit.

P.I.O.N.E.E.R.

P - Persistence in Building Community and Mining:

In the vast landscape of the Pi Network, the pioneers who have remained steadfast in their journey know the true essence of persistence. They understand that just as a tiny drop of water can carve a mighty canyon over time, their consistent efforts hold the power to shape the future of Pi.

Imagine you are a determined gardener tending to a seed you planted with hope and anticipation. At first, you water it diligently, nurturing it with care. But as time goes on, the sun's scorching rays and life's demands start to weigh on you. Doubts creep in, and you wonder if the seed will ever bloom into a magnificent tree.

Yet, deep within, you know that nature's wonders take time to unfold. So, you choose to embrace the PIONEER spirit, understanding that greatness is not achieved overnight. With unwavering resolve, you continue to water the seed, knowing that your persistence will yield the sweetest fruit.

Similarly, clicking that mining button every 24 hours demands persistence and consistency. At times, it may seem like a small action, but like the steady drops of water nurturing the seed, each click accumulates into something extraordinary. Each click strengthens the foundation of the Pi Network, contributing to its growth and resilience.

To those pioneers who may have grown weary, I urge you not to lose hope. Imagine your mining button as a dazzling lightning bolt, crackling with potential. With every click, you send a surge of energy through the network, illuminating the path to a brighter future. Remember, it is not the first flash that shapes the sky, but the continuous strikes that create the most spectacular storms.

So, in the face of challenges and doubts, click that lightning button with renewed determination. Your consistency becomes the beacon that lights the way for others, inspiring them to follow your lead. Embrace the PIONEER spirit, for it is through persistence and unwavering dedication that the most extraordinary visions come to life.

I - Invest in Knowledge and Understanding:

In the realm of Pi Network, knowledge is a potent elixir. To truly embrace the PIONEER spirit, we must invest in understanding the technology that powers our journey. We delve into the workings of blockchain, grasp the principles of consensus mechanisms, and comprehend the mechanisms that secure our transactions. Armed with this knowledge, we become guardians of our own destiny, avoiding the pitfalls of ignorance that may lead to folly. It's upon this principal this book has been written.

O - Overcoming Impatience:

In a world where everything is at our fingertips, the virtue of patience can be elusive. The PIONEER spirit calls for overcoming impatience, for Rome was not built in a day, and neither will the Pi Network achieve its full potential overnight. We must recognize that true success comes to those who endure the tests of time, weathering storms and standing strong in the face of challenges. The Pi Network is a long-term endeavor, and embracing this reality fortifies our resilience.

N - Nurture Long-Term Vision:

The PIONEER spirit thrives on a long-term vision that stretches far beyond the horizon. We must resist the siren call of get-rich-quick schemes and instead nurture a vision of sustainable growth. The Pi Network seeks to be a pillar of trust, a beacon of fairness, and a catalyst for positive change in the world of cryptocurrencies. As pioneers, we cultivate this vision, tending to its growth with care and determination.

E - Embrace Effort and Hard Work:

In the grand tapestry of the Pi Network, there are no shortcuts to success. The PIONEER spirit embraces effort and hard work as the threads that weave our story. We actively participate in the mining process, contribute to the network's security, and engage in activities that add value to the community which include participation in Hackathons, Using applications on pi ecosystem, recruiting members. Like a blacksmith forging steel, we mold our destinies through diligence and dedication.

E - Earning Pi every day, the true Pioneer Spirit urges one to diligently click the lightning button to restart a mining session, a very important assignment in the routine of a pioneer. It is an easy task that has the potential to revolutionize the internet.

R - Realize the True Value

As pioneers of the Pi Network, we are called upon to see beyond the surface, to grasp the true value that lies within the heart of Pi. It is not merely a fleeting figure on a market chart; it is a beacon of change and progress.

Imagine Pi as a shimmering gem hidden within the depths of a rugged terrain. Its brilliance is not fully realized until it is unearthed and polished to perfection. In the same way, the true value of Pi is created through the process of unearthing its potential, shaping it into utilities applications, and nurturing a thriving community to embrace and utilize them.

The PIONEER spirit encourages us to understand that the real value of Pi emerges from the creation of these utilities applications and the collective effort to make them an integral part of our daily lives. It is in building a robust ecosystem, where these applications serve as bridges that connect individuals, facilitate transactions, and foster economic empowerment.

Beyond the lure of speculative gains, Pi embodies the principles of fairness, inclusivity, and empowerment. It is a token of trust, a symbol of a united community striving towards a shared vision. Each transaction, each connection, each interaction adds another facet to the gem, enhancing its brilliance.

As pioneers, we are the architects of Pi's true value. The bonds we forge, the friendships we kindle, and the unity we foster are the precious threads that weave the tapestry of its worth. Our dedication to creating and utilizing utilities applications in our daily lives gives Pi a purpose and meaning that extends far beyond the realm of digital currency.

In conclusion, dear pioneers, let us embrace the PIONEER spirit with open hearts and resolute minds. Together, we embark on a journey that transcends the allure of quick, easy, and free money. Instead, we tread the path of perseverance, knowledge, patience, vision, effort, and the recognition of true value. As we embrace the PIONEER spirit, we become torchbearers of a brighter tomorrow, shaping the Pi Network into a force for positive change in the world of cryptocurrencies.

Chapter 8: Pi Network White Paper Summary

A CRYPTOCURRENCY WHITE Paper is a document that outlines the technical and economic aspects of a new cryptocurrency or blockchain project. It is typically written by the project's developers or founders and is intended to provide potential investors and users with information about the project.

It's important to Note, Pi White Paper Summary is intended to give you overview of the project. The actual content and structure of the Pi Network's white paper will furnish you with details and you will be able to comprehend nitty gritty of the project. For the most accurate and up-to-date information, I recommend referring to the official Pi Network website to read the White Paper.

We will summarize the Pi White Paper content in this form. However we will omit parts and details covered elsewhere in this book.

1.Introduction: This section introduces the Pi project, its goals, and the problems it aims to solve.

2. Technical Overview: Here, we delve into Pi's underlying technology and the consensus mechanism that the network employs.

3.Token Economics: This section covers the details of the Pi's native token, including its distribution, supply, and use cases within the ecosystem.

4. Mining and Validation: It explains the process of how new tokens are minted or mined and the rules for validating transactions.

5. Community and Governance: This part describes how the community is involved in decision-making and how governance issues are handled.

6. Use Cases and Applications: The white paper highlights potential use cases and real-world applications of the cryptocurrency.

7. Roadmap and Future Development: It outlines the project's milestones, development plans, and the vision for the future.

8. Team and Partners: This section introduces the core team members, advisors, and strategic partners involved in the project.

9. Security and Privacy: It addresses the security measures taken to safeguard the network and user data.

10. Legal and Regulatory Compliance: The white paper may discuss the project's approach to comply with relevant legal and regulatory frameworks.

1. Introduction:

Mission: Build a cryptocurrency and smart contracts platform secured and operated by everyday people.

Vision: Build the world's most inclusive peer-to-peer ecosystem and online experience, fueled by Pi, the world's most widely used cryptocurrency

Defining The Problem:

Currently, our financial transactions heavily rely on trusted intermediaries like banks and PayPal to record and guarantee the safety of these transactions. These intermediaries play a crucial role in regulating the world's financial activities. However, they also have limitations that affect everyday people:

1. Unfair Value Capture: Trusted intermediaries accumulate enormous wealth (e.g., PayPal's market cap is ~$130B) but offer minimal benefits to their customers, who are the driving force behind the global economy. This wealth disparity leaves many individuals behind.

2. Fees: Banks and companies charge significant fees for facilitating transactions, disproportionately impacting lower-income populations with fewer alternatives.

3. Censorship: Trusted intermediaries can restrict the movement of money if they deem it necessary, leading to potential limitations on financial freedom.

4. Permissioned: Acting as gatekeepers, these intermediaries can arbitrarily deny access to their networks, limiting financial inclusion.

5. Pseudonymous: Concerns over privacy arise as powerful intermediaries may unintentionally or intentionally disclose more financial information than users desire, compromising their privacy.

Bitcoin' s Distributed Ledger

Bitcoin utilizes a distributed ledger system to record transactions, ensuring transparency and preventing fraud. To address security challenges in maintaining this open and editable ledger, Bitcoin introduced a process called Mining, using the consensus algorithm "Proof of Work." Mining is like an economic game where Validators compete to prove their worth by solving complex computational puzzles. The first Validator to solve the puzzle is rewarded with the opportunity to add the latest block of transactions, earning a Block Reward. This approach ensures the integrity and trustworthiness of the distributed ledger.

Bitcoin Problem

The centralization of power and wealth in 1st Generation Cryptocurrencies, like Bitcoin, has become a significant problem. The ease of mining Bitcoin led to the rise of mining farms, resulting in a concentration of production power and wealth in the hands of a few. Currently, 87% of all Bitcoins are owned by only 1% of the network, with many of these coins obtained nearly free in the early days of mining. For the average person, acquiring Bitcoin has become challenging and costly due to this centralization of power. The options available are either mining or buying the cryptocurrency.

Pi Network aims to close the divide in cryptocurrency accessibility by simplifying the technology, enabling anyone with a smartphone to mine Pi for free. This approach eliminates the cost barrier often associated with cryptocurrency adoption.

Second, a limitation of cryptocurrencies has been their lack of utilities. Cryptocurrencies have not been widely adopted for use in everyday transactions, like fiat currency. This has led to cryptocurrencies being reduced to instruments of speculation, which has had detrimental effects on the volatility of crypto prices. Pi intends to bridge this gap by having utility apps built into its ecosystem, which the community will use to spend their Pi.

2. Technical Overview:

Solution: Pi - Enabling mining on mobile phones

The Pi Core Team recognized the barriers to cryptocurrency adoption and sought a solution that would allow ordinary individuals to mine and earn rewards for validating transactions on a distributed ledger. To achieve this, they aimed to design a consensus algorithm that is user-friendly and supports mining on personal computers and mobile phones.

After evaluating various consensus algorithms, the Stellar Consensus Protocol (SCP) emerged as the leading candidate. SCP, architected by David Mazières, a professor of Computer Science at Stanford and Chief Scientist at the Stellar Development Foundation, employs Federated Byzantine Agreements to ensure accurate and trustworthy updates to the distributed ledger. This protocol has been successfully operating on the Stellar blockchain since 2015 and is seen as the ideal choice for enabling user-friendly and mobile-first mining on the Pi network.

Pi users can play four different roles as Pi miners:

(i) Pioneer: These users validate their presence in the Pi mobile app daily, confirming that they are not automated bots. They can also initiate transactions, such as making payments in Pi to other pioneers.

(ii) Contributor: Pi contributors use the mobile app to provide a list of pioneers they know and trust. By aggregating this information, Pi contributors collectively build a global trust graph.

(iii) Ambassador: Ambassadors are Pi mobile app users who actively introduce and onboard new users into the Pi network.

(iv) Node: Nodes are users who fulfill multiple roles. They are pioneers and contributors using the Pi mobile app while also running the Pi node software on their desktop or laptop computers. The Pi node software is crucial for running the core SCP algorithm and incorporates the trust graph information provided by contributors.

3. Token Economics:

i. Distribution: The Pi Network will be distributed to users over a period of several years. The initial distribution will be based on a user's contribution to the network. Users can earn Pi by participating in the network, such as by verifying transactions, building apps, and promoting the network.

ii. Supply: The total supply of Pi is capped at 100 billion. This means that there will never be more than 100 billion Pi in circulation. Community will receive 80% and Core team 20%. Community's share is further dividend: 65% will be available for pioneers to mine. 10% of Pi will go towards Pi foundation which will be non profit organization helping in deleloping community applications and 5% of will be liquidity pool to Pioneers and Developers on Pi ecosystem.

iii. Use cases: Pi will be used within the Pi Network ecosystem for a variety of purposes, such as:

a. Payments: Pi can be used to make payments for goods and services within the Pi Network ecosystem.

b. Locking Pi : Pi can be locked to increase mining rate.

iv. Scarcity: The Pi Network uses a logarithmically declining mining rate, which means that the rate at which Pi can be mined will decrease over time. This will create scarcity and increase the value of Pi.

The Pi Network token economics are designed to be fair and equitable. The distribution of Pi is based on a user's contribution to the network, which ensures that users who are most active in the network will be rewarded the most. The capped supply of Pi also ensures that there will never be an unlimited supply of Pi, which will help to maintain its value.

4. Mining and Validation:

Pioneers earn Pi tokens by contributing to the growth, distribution, and security of the network.

The more a Pioneer contributes, the higher their reputation score, which means they can mine more Pi.

Pioneers can earn a reputation score by building a Security Circle, maintaining an active Pi app, and participating in Pi Network activities.

The Pi mining process is designed to be fair and accessible to everyone.

In simple terms, the more you contribute to the Pi Network, the more Pi you will earn. The Pi mining process is designed to be fair and accessible to everyone, so anyone with a mobile phone can participate.

5. Community and Governance:

Pi holders will be able to participate in the governance of the Pi Network by voting.

i. The Pi Core Team: The Pi Core Team is responsible for the development and maintenance of the Pi Network. The team is made up of experienced engineers and entrepreneurs who are committed to building a fair and accessible cryptocurrency for everyone.

ii. The Pi Foundation: The Pi Foundation is a non-profit organization that is responsible for overseeing the governance of the Pi Network. The foundation is made up of representatives from the Pi Core Team, the Pi community, and other stakeholders.

iii. The Pi Community: The Pi Community is the heart of the Pi Network. The community is made up of Pioneers from all over the world who are committed to building a better financial system. The community is involved in all aspects of the Pi Network, from mining and validating transactions to developing new features.

There is anticipation of two-tiered governance system on Pi Network:

i. On-chain governance:

On-chain governance refers to the process of making decisions about the Pi Network through the use of smart contracts. This type of governance is transparent and democratic, as it allows all Pioneers to participate in the decision-making process.

ii. Off-chain governance: Off-chain governance refers to the process of making decisions about the Pi Network through the use of traditional institutions, such as the Pi Foundation. This type of governance is more centralized, but it can be more efficient and effective in making decisions that require specialized knowledge or expertise.

The Pi Network white paper states that the goal is to eventually transition to a fully on-chain governance system. However, the team recognizes that the Pi Network is still in its early stages, and that off-chain governance may be necessary for the time being.

6. Use Cases and Applications:

The Pi Network white paper envisions the following use cases and applications for the cryptocurrency:

i. Micro-transactions: Pi can be used for small, everyday transactions, such as buying a cup of coffee or tipping a content creator.

ii. Peer-to-peer payments: Pi can be used to send and receive payments directly between users, without the need for a third party.

iii. Online shopping: Pi can be used to purchase goods and services from online merchants.

iv. Donations: Pi can be used to donate to charities or other causes.

iv. Locking: Pi can be locked to earn rewards.

v. Governance: Pi holders can vote on proposals that affect the future of the network.

The white paper also envisions the development of a variety of Pi-based applications, such as:

A social media platform that rewards users for their attention.

A marketplace where users can buy and sell goods and services.

A crowdfunding platform that allows users to raise money for projects.

A microloan platform that provides small loans to entrepreneurs.

The white paper acknowledges that these are just a few of the potential use cases for Pi. The ultimate success of the project will depend on the creativity and innovation of the Pi community.

7. Roadmap and Future Development:

Phase 1: Beta

The beta phase was successfully carried out. In this phase, the Pi Network was being developed and tested. The goal of the beta phase was to build a large and active community of users and to test the security and scalability of the network.

Phase 2: Testnet

The testnet phase followed the beta phase. In this phase, the Pi Network was partially decentralized and open to Pi Network community participation. The goal of the testnet phase is to test the network under real-world conditions and to gather feedback from the community.

Phase 3: Mainnet

The mainnet phase followed the testnet phase. In this phase, the Pi Network will be fully launched and will be available for commercial use. The goal of the mainnet phase is to create a decentralized and scalable cryptocurrency that can be used for everyday transactions.

Closed Mainnet: Pi Network is currently in this phase by the time of writing this book.

The closed mainnet phase of Pi Network is a period in which the Pi Network blockchain is active but is not yet fully accessible to the public.

This phase is designed to allow the Pi Network team to test and improve the network before it is opened to the general public.

During the closed mainnet phase, Pi Network users can continue to mine Pi, but they cannot trade or exchange their Pi for fiat currency or other cryptocurrencies. Additionally, the Pi Network blockchain is not yet connected to other blockchains, so Pi cannot be used to make payments on other platforms.

The closed mainnet phase is expected to last for several months, after which the Pi Network will transition to the open mainnet phase. The open mainnet phase will mark the full launch of the Pi Network and will allow Pi to be used for all of its intended purposes.

8. Team and Partners:

The Pi Network white paper anticipates how the team and partners will achieve the project's goals by outlining the following key points:

Here are some of the specific ways in which the team and partners plan to achieve the project's goals:

i. The core team: The core team will continue to develop the Pi Network's technology and infrastructure. They will also work to expand the Pi Network's community and reach a wider audience.

ii. The advisors: The advisors will provide guidance and support to the core team on a variety of topics, including security, regulation, and marketing. They will also help the core team to navigate the challenges facing the cryptocurrency industry.

iii. The strategic partners: The strategic partners will help the Pi Network to develop and launch the project. They will also provide access to their networks and resources, which will help the Pi Network to reach a wider audience and achieve its goals.

9. Security and Privacy:

The Pi Network white paper addresses the security measures taken to safeguard the network and user data in detail:

Security: The Pi Network uses a number of security measures to protect the network and user data. These measures include:

i. Cryptography: The Pi Network uses cryptography to secure the network and user data. This includes the use of public-key cryptography to encrypt data and digital signatures to verify transactions.

ii. Decentralization: The Pi Network is a decentralized network. This means that there is no central authority that controls the network. This makes it more difficult for attackers to compromise the network.

iii. Security Circles: Pi users are encouraged to form Security Circles. Security Circles are groups of users who trust each other. This helps to protect the network by making it more difficult for attackers to gain access to user data.

Privacy: The Pi Network team is committed to protecting user privacy. The team has taken a number of steps to protect user privacy, including:

(i) Data minimization: The Pi Network team only collects the data that is necessary to operate the network.

(ii) Data anonymization: The Pi Network team anonymizes user data before it is stored or transmitted. Data anonymization is the process of removing or altering personally identifiable information (PII) from data sets so that the people whom the data describe remain anonymous. This is done to protect the privacy of individuals and to prevent the misuse of their data.

(iii) User control: Users have control over their data. Users can choose to share their data with the Pi Network team, or they can choose to keep their data private.

The Pi Network team is committed to providing a secure and private platform for users to mine and use Pi. The team is constantly working to improve the security and privacy of the Pi Network.

Here are some additional thoughts on the security and privacy of Pi:

The Pi Network is still in its early stages of development, so the security measures may not be as robust as they will be in the future. The team is constantly working to improve the security of the Pi Network, and they are committed to providing a secure platform for users.

Users should be aware of the risks associated with using any cryptocurrency, including Pi. These risks include the possibility of fraud, theft, and loss. Users should take steps to protect their Pi, such as storing it in a secure wallet. Without sharing their wallet details with any other person.

The security and privacy of Pi are important considerations for users. The Pi Network team is committed to providing a secure and private platform for users to mine and use Pi.

10. Legal and Regulatory:

Compliance: The Pi Network team is committed to complying with all applicable laws and regulations. The team has a legal team that is responsible for reviewing and updating the Pi Network's compliance policies.

i. KYC/AML: The Pi Network team is committed to implementing KYC/AML procedures. KYC/AML stands for Know Your Customer/Anti-Money Laundering. These procedures are designed to prevent the use of Pi for illegal activities.

ii. Taxes: The Pi Network team is committed to complying with all applicable tax laws. The team will provide users with information about how to report their Pi holdings and earnings on their taxes.

iii. Regulatory sandbox: The Pi Network team is working with regulators to participate in a regulatory sandbox. A regulatory sandbox is a controlled environment where new products and services can be tested without the full regulatory burden. This will help the Pi Network team to comply with regulations and to get feedback from regulators.

The Pi Network team is committed to complying with all applicable laws and regulations. The team is working with regulators to ensure that Pi is a compliant cryptocurrency.

Here are some additional thoughts on the legal and regulatory compliance of Pi:

The legal and regulatory landscape for cryptocurrencies is constantly evolving. The Pi Network team is committed to staying up-to-date on the latest regulations and to complying with all applicable laws.

Users should be aware of the risks associated with using any cryptocurrency, including Pi. These risks include the possibility of regulatory changes that could affect the value of Pi.

The legal and regulatory compliance of Pi is an important consideration for users. The Pi Network team is committed to providing a compliant cryptocurrency platform for users.

Chapter 9: Pi Network, Not a Pump and Dump Project

IN THE WORLD OF CRYPTOCURRENCIES, one term that often raises eyebrows and invokes suspicion is "pump and dump." This chapter delves into the concept of pump and dump and emphasizes how Pi Network distinguishes itself as a legitimate and community-driven project.

Ah, my dear reader, brace yourself for the wild and treacherous world of cryptocurrencies, where a term like "pump and dump" is as shady as a ninja in the dark. It's the kind of strategy that makes you raise an eyebrow and say, "Who do they think they are, pulling off these sneaky maneuvers?"

Understanding Pump and Dump:

"Pump and dump" is a deceptive and manipulative trading strategy commonly observed in the cryptocurrency market, though it can occur in other financial markets as well. The process involves artificially inflating the price of a particular asset (pumping) by spreading false or exaggerated information to attract buyers. Once the price rises significantly, the manipulators swiftly sell off their holdings (dumping) at a profit, leaving unsuspecting investors with substantial losses.

Examples of Pump and Dump:

1. Shady Token X:

Imagine a situation where a group of individuals creates a new cryptocurrency token called "Token X." They hype up Token X on social media platforms, claiming it to be the "next big thing" in the crypto space. They spread rumors of potential partnerships with well-known companies, upcoming revolutionary features, and exponential price growth that would make even James Bond jealous. As a result, many investors, driven by FOMO (fear of missing out), rush to buy Token X, thinking they've struck gold, causing its price to skyrocket rapidly. Once the price reaches a peak, the manipulators sell their holdings, causing a massive price crash, and leaving investors with substantial losses. Many investors have been caught in this financial rollercoaster.

2. Fake Exchange Listing:

Now, let me paint you another scene. Imagine a group of merry bandits creating their own crypto project and boldly declaring that a prominent exchange will list their token. They use this misinformation to attract investors who hope to benefit from the potential price surge when the token is listed. Once the rumor has fueled enough buying activity, the manipulators sell their holdings, causing the token's value to plummet. The exchange never had any intentions of listing their token, and when the truth hits the fan, these sneaky schemers vanish into thin air, leaving investors with wallets as light as feathers

But fear not, my friends, for here comes the shining knight in the crypto realm - the Pi Network! It's not just another crypto project; it's the bright beacon of hope, guided by a community-driven approach that would make Robin Hood himself proud.

Pi Network's Distinction:

The Pi Network differentiates itself from pump and dump schemes in several key ways:

1. Community-Driven Approach:

Pi Network's inception was based on the idea of creating a cryptocurrency accessible to the masses. Picture a merry band of crypto enthusiasts mining away on their mobile devices, making the process so simple that even your grandma could do it with one eye closed. The Pi Network ensures that everyone gets a slice of the pie, avoiding the hoarding antics of those pump and dump pirates.The project relies on a growing community of users who mine Pi tokens through the mobile app. The app's mining process is designed to be user-friendly and energy-efficient, ensuring that participants are genuinely contributing to the network's growth.

2. Fair Distribution:

Unlike pump and dump schemes that often concentrate wealth in the hands of a few manipulators, Pi Network aims to achieve fair distribution of its tokens. By implementing an invitation-based system early on, the project sought to avoid hoarding and centralization and ensure that more people could participate in the mining process. Furthermore they're building an ecosystem, a land of crypto opportunity, where everyone can reap the rewards and bask in the glory of fairness and sustainability

3. Long-Term Vision:

Let me tell you, the folks behind Pi Network aren't just sailing the high seas of crypto without a compass. Oh no! They've got a vision, a long-term vision that extends beyond the horizon, where quick profits are like fleeting shooting star.

Pi Network has a long-term vision for its development and adoption. Rather than promising quick profits or exaggerated returns, the project emphasizes building a sustainable ecosystem that benefits all its participants.

4. Transparency and Accountability:

Transparency, my dear reader, is their battle cry! The core team at Pi Network stands tall, waving the flag of openness and accountability. They don't hide behind closed doors like those shady pump and dump dealers. Oh no, they share their plans, progress, and challenges with the community, sparking trust like a campfire on a chilly night.

So, there you have it, my fellow adventurers! Pi Network is the hero of the crypto saga, fighting the good fight against pump and dump villains. Remember, though, always do your research and tread carefully in this crypto wilderness. But with Pi Network's community-driven spirit, fair distribution, long-term vision, and transparency, you might just find yourself sailing on the high seas of crypto success with a crew of true pioneers!.

Conclusion:

Pi Network is a project that aims to be a genuinely community-driven and sustainable cryptocurrency platform. It stands in stark contrast to pump and dump schemes that exploit investor sentiments for short-term gains. By fostering a supportive and inclusive community and focusing on fair distribution, long-term vision, and transparency, Pi Network demonstrates its commitment to being a legitimate and credible player in the cryptocurrency space. As with any investment or project, individuals are encouraged to conduct their research and exercise caution, but Pi Network's distinguishing features provide reasons to believe in its potential for a more equitable and user-friendly digital currency system.

Part III: Pi Development

Chapter 10: Pi Browser - Unleashing the Realm of Applications

IN THE VAST AND ENCHANTING realm of Pi Network lies the Pi Browser, a portal to a world of diverse applications created both by the core team and the vibrant community of pioneers. As you enter this mystical gateway, prepare to be enthralled by the wonders that await you.

Applications Built by the Core Team:

1. KYC - Ensuring Authenticity:

Within the Pi Browser, the first stop is the KYC (Know Your Customer) application. Here, the core team wields the combined power of machines and human oversight to ensure that every pioneer is a real person and that no one possesses the privilege of holding multiple accounts. Through biometric features and identification document verification, the KYC process upholds the integrity and security of the Pi Network.

2. Pi Wallet - The Treasure Keeper:

Next, you encounter the Pi Wallet, a non-custodian haven where the Pi tokens earned from mining are securely stored. This remarkable wallet empowers each pioneer with control over their assets by allowing them to hold their private keys independently. It's like a magic chest, safeguarding your tokens while granting you the freedom to manage and transfer them with ease.

Non-Custodian Security:

Picture this wallet as a magic vault that only you hold the key to. Unlike traditional custodian wallets where third parties hold your assets, the Pi Wallet empowers you with full control. Your private keys reside safely with you, shielding your tokens from the prying eyes of any unsavory characters.

- Seamless Transactions:

Sending and receiving Pi tokens becomes a breeze with the Pi Wallet. Like a teleportation spell, you can effortlessly send tokens to friends, family, or anyone in the Pi Network with just a few taps on your device. No intermediaries, no delays – just swift and secure transactions.

- Accessible Across Platforms:

Whether you're a wizard with a smartphone or a Guru with a desktop, fear not, for the Pi Wallet is designed to be accessible on multiple platforms. It accompanies you wherever your crypto journey takes you, allowing you to manage your Pi tokens with ease.

- Locking Pi and Earning Rewards:

But wait, there's more! The Pi Wallet isn't just a guardian of your Pi tokens; it also opens doors to exciting possibilities. With the power of staking, you can contribute to the security of the network and earn additional Pi tokens as a reward for your loyalty.

3. Chat App - Fostering Connections:

In the whimsical world of Pi Network, communication is key, and the Chat App bridges the gaps between pioneers. Through this social avenue, you can connect with like-minded individuals, share ideas, and immerse yourself in the spirit of camaraderie.

4. Brainstorm App - Nurturing Creativity:

Ah, the Brainstorm App! Here, pioneers can freely unleash their ideas and visions, connecting with developers and thinkers alike. It's a place of inspiration, where creativity knows no bounds, and innovation finds its roots.

5. Blockchain Pi - Illuminating Transparency:

As you delve deeper into the Pi Browser, the Blockchain Pi application awaits. Here, the blockchain's transparency shines brightly, revealing all transactions ever conducted within the Pi Network. This open book allows pioneers to witness the flow of Pi tokens, ensuring a trustworthy and transparent ecosystem.

6. Developed Pi - Empowering Developers:

For those with the heart of a builder, the Developed Pi application opens doors to endless possibilities. Developers can access open-source tools and software development kits (SDKs) to bring their projects to life and contribute to the Pi Network's continuous growth.

7. Fireside - Igniting Social Rewards:

Last but not least, the core team has recently kindled a new social media platform called Fireside. Pioneers gather around the digital fireplace, sharing content and earning Fire Coins as they spread the warmth of knowledge, laughter, and camaraderie.

Exploring the Testnet Ecosystem:

Beyond the core team's creations, the Pi Browser ventures further into the Testnet Ecosystem, a realm where community applications reside, either in the testing phase or on the mainnet, fully operational and thriving.

Applications on Mainnet:

1. Chain Mall for Pi - Embracing E-commerce:

Enter the bustling streets of Chain Mall for Pi, an enchanting e-commerce platform where pioneers can indulge in a diverse array of products using Pi coins. It's a marketplace where both buyers and sellers revel in the magic of blockchain-enabled transactions.

2. The Pitogo Travel - Wanderlust Meets Pi:

Prepare to set off on an adventure with The Pitogo Travel. This social media platform doubles as a hub for travel services, offering transportation, accommodation, and hospitality options that pioneers can access and pay for with Pi tokens. Wanderlust meets the power of cryptocurrency, and a world of exploration awaits.

3. Workforcepool - Empowering Freelancers:

In the realm of Workforcepool, a digital oasis connects freelancers with employers in need of their skills. Pi tokens emerge as a means of payment, fostering a seamless and borderless labor market, where talents meet opportunities.

As you traverse the rich landscapes of the Pi Browser, you discover an ecosystem brimming with potential, fueled by the collective creativity and dedication of pioneers. From applications built by the core team to the vibrant offerings of the community, Pi Network's browser is a gateway to a realm where possibilities bloom like stars in the night sky. So, venture forth, dear pioneer, and embrace the magic that awaits in the Pi Browser!

Chapter 11: Pi Hackathons: Unbounded Benefits to Pioneers

A HACKATHON IS A DESIGN sprint-like event in which computer programmers and others involved in software development, including graphic designers, interface designers, product managers, project managers, domain experts, and others collaborate intensively on software projects. It is a portmanteau of hacking and marathon.

The main objective of a hackathon is to create functioning software or hardware by the end of the event. Hackathons tend to have a specific focus, which can include the programming language used, the operating system, an application, an API, or the subject and the demographic group of the programmers.

Pi Network has held two hackathons so far, in 2021 and 2023. The hackathons are designed to encourage developers to build applications on the Pi Network platform. The winners of the hackathons receive prizes in the form of Pi cryptocurrency tokens and other rewards.

Objectives of the hackathons:

The objectives of the Pi hackathons are to:

* Encourage developers to build applications on the Pi Network platform.

* Promote the development of the Pi Network ecosystem.

* Reward developers for their contributions to the Pi Network.

The Pi Hackathon is a great opportunity for Pioneers to benefit in a number of ways. Here are some of the key benefits:

Learn new skills: The Hackathon will provide Pioneers with the opportunity to learn new skills in blockchain development, app development, and other areas. This will help them to become more valuable members of the Pi Network community and to contribute to the development of the Pi ecosystem.

Meet new people: The Hackathon will be a great opportunity for Pioneers to meet new people from all over the world who are interested in blockchain technology. This will help them to build relationships with other developers and to learn from their experiences.

Build cool stuff:The Hackathon will provide Pioneers with the opportunity to build cool stuff using the Pi Network platform. This could include anything from simple apps to complex dApps. This will help them to showcase their skills and to make a real contribution to the Pi ecosystem.

Win prizes: There will be a number of prizes up for grabs at the Hackathon, including Pi, merchandise, and other rewards. This will provide Pioneers with an incentive to participate and to create their best work.

Overall, the Pi Hackathon is a great opportunity for Pioneers to learn new skills, meet new people, build cool stuff, and win prizes. I encourage all Pioneers who are interested in blockchain development to participate.

Here are some additional benefits that Pioneers can expect from the Pi Hackathon:

Access to the Pi SDK: The Pi SDK(Software Development Kit). Will provide Pioneers with the tools they need to build Pi apps. This will make it easier for them to develop and deploy their apps on the Pi Network platform.

Support from the Pi Core Team: The Pi Core Team will be providing support to Pioneers throughout the Hackathon. This will include providing guidance on how to use the Pi SDK, answering questions, and helping to troubleshoot problems.

A chance to make a real impact on the Pi ecosystem: The Hackathon will provide Pioneers with the opportunity to build apps that will be used by millions of people around the world. This is a chance to make a real impact on the world and to help to shape the future of blockchain technology.

Winners of the first hackathon 2021:

Pi Workforce Pool (#1 business app)

Marketplace to hire skilled Pioneers or get hired for work

PiCare (#1 ecosystem app)

Bug reporting platform for Pi apps and ecosystem apps

Pi Chain Mall (#2 business app)

E-commerce marketplace for buyers and sellers of various goods and services

World of Pi Championships (#2 ecosystem app)

Social match-three puzzle game to compete for prizes — non-profit for the developer.

Watugot (#3 business app)

Marketplace for local businesses to publish their coupons and discounts

Honorable mentions:

Pi Game Platform (business app)

Platform for developers to post and monetize their games

Pi Barter Mall (business app)

E-commerce Marketplace for buyers and sellers of various physical and virtual goods.

PitoGo Travelers Handy Platform (business app)

Travel platform to book arrangements including hotels, flights, and cars.

Pi Webinars (business model app)

Video platform to sell and buy exclusive content.

Pi Games from Latin America (ecosystem app)

Numerous games including chess against an AI chess bot. All code is open-source.

2023 Hackathon Winners

Overall Winner

Polls for Pi: a Web3.0 polling app that designs and administers polls and surveys, where the poll poster pays Pioneers for their answers to their polls in Pi

Overall Runner-Up Winners

Connect Social: a social media Testnet app built for Pioneers to engage, learn, and have some fun with each other

Coinskro: an escrow app that addresses a current need in the network and includes a disputes resolution mechanism to enable secure and trusted peer-to-peer or business-to-Pioneer bartering of Pi for goods and services.

Piketplace: a peer-to-peer marketplace app with a clean and accessible user interface and translations in multiple languages that is on the Testnet.

Category Winners

Social Media:

BBS Chat

BBS Chat is a social forum for Pioneers with a good Pi integration, which allows Pi tipping to posters and a Pi paywall to access full content if a poster so chooses. This Mainnet social media app has a clean user interface design, especially compared to some of the other apps in the same category. It also enables Pioneers to select and explore posts within their stated interests

Games and Entertainment:

Pet for Pi

Pet for Pi is a pet-cultivating game where Pioneers can collect, breed, and trade virtual 'pets' with other members using Pi, and improve their pet's vitality score by taking care of them. The developers envision these Pets becoming NFTs. This idle game with good graphics design and its in-game economy, currently on their Testnet app, is a great use case for Pi.

Open Innovation:

Voice of Pi

Voice of Pi is another PiOS app that blends social and marketplace features into one app. Currently on the Testnet, Voice of Pi leverages Pi tipping and payments. Most notably, in a stellar demonstration of the collaborative spirit of Pioneers, dozens of other hackathon submissions were built on top of Voice of Pi's app framework, thanks to the accessible nature of PiOS. These various apps, available across multiple languages, are instantiations of its core app in different verticals of market or regions, enabling local merchants to offer a virtual storefront for Pioneers and create sub communities around their businesses

VC Judging Round

Explore

ExplorePi is a Mainnet block explorer app with a clear user interface, making Pi blockchain data easy to access and understand with helpful visuals and interactive graphs.

Honorable Mentions

Neobot: an AI chatbot

Door for Pi: a Pi block explorer

App.Link for Pi: a collection of various Pi Apps reviewed and rated by the community

Quotline: a social app to share and engage with quotes

Pi Fruit: an idle game with Pi-based in-game economy

Youpi: a marketplace where users can buy goods with Pi

DAO Mall: a marketplace built on a One-Stop Comprehensive Ecological City

Store on Pi: a marketplace that brings together global physical stores

Daabia Shopping Mall: a marketplace delivering a multi-vendor ecommerce experience

The future of Pi hackathons

Pi Network plans to hold hackathons on a regular basis. The hackathons will help to grow the Pi Network ecosystem and encourage developers to build innovative applications on the Pi Network platform.

Conclusion

The Pi hackathons have been a great success. They have encouraged developers to build applications on the Pi Network platform and have promoted the development of the Pi Network ecosystem. The hackathons will continue to be held on a regular basis, and they will play an important role in the future of the Pi Network.

Information from

https://minepi.com/blog/hackathon-winners-2023

https://minepi.com/blog/hackathon-winners-announcement

Chapter 12: Closed & Open Pi Mainnet

The closed mainnet started from June 2022 when Pioneer's mined pi started to be migrated to Mainnet for those who had already passed KYC. Closed mainnet allows Pioneers to migrate their mined Pi to the mainnet and start using it to transact with each other. However, the closed mainnet has a firewall that prevents it from being accessed by the public. This is to give the Pi team time to mature some of the applications that will be built on top of the Pi network before opening it up to the public.

The open mainnet will be a fully functional blockchain that anyone can access other blockchain will be able to connect. It will allow Pioneers to send and receive Pi, use it to buy goods and services, and participate in decentralized applications. The Pi team plans to open the open mainnet once the application utilities matures and are fully tested for mass adoption.

Here are some of the benefits of having a closed mainnet:

* It allows the Pi team to test the network and make sure that it is stable and secure before opening it up to the public.

* It allows the Pi team to mature some of the applications that will be built on top of the Pi network.

* It allows the Pi team to collect data on how the network is being used and make adjustments as needed.

Here are some of the challenges of having a closed mainnet:

* It can be frustrating for Pioneers who want to use Pi to transact with each other.

* It can be difficult for developers to build applications on top of the Pi network if they cannot access the full functionality of the network.

* It can be difficult for the Pi team to get feedback from the public on how the network is working.

Overall, the closed mainnet is a necessary step in the development of the Pi network. It allows the Pi team to test the network and make sure that it is ready for the public. It also allows the Pi team to mature some of the applications that will be built on top of the Pi network.

During the closed mainnet, Pioneers can transfer Pi among themselves on the blockchain, and they can also use Pi to buy goods and services from participating merchants. However, they cannot exchange Pi for fiat currency or other cryptocurrencies. This is because the closed mainnet is still in a testing phase, and the Pi team wants to make sure that the Pi network is stable and secure before it is opened up to the public.

Once the open mainnet is launched, Pioneers will be able to exchange Pi for fiat currency and other cryptocurrencies. They will also be able to use Pi to participate in a wider range of decentralized applications.

Part IV: Unlimited Opportunities in Pi Network

Chapter 13: Pi Network - A Web 3 Leader, Unleashing the Wealth of the Internet to All Users

UNDERSTANDING WEB 3:

Web 3, also known as the decentralized web or the semantic web, represents the next evolutionary phase of the internet. It is a vision of the internet that aims to overcome the limitations and shortcomings of the current centralized web (Web 2) by leveraging blockchain technology and decentralization principles. Web 3 envisions an internet where data ownership, privacy, and security are prioritized, empowering users to have more control over their digital identities and assets.

At the core of Web 3 lies the idea of decentralized applications (dApps) running on blockchain networks. These dApps eliminate the need for intermediaries, such as tech giants and data brokers, by using smart contracts and consensus mechanisms for transactions and data validation. This not only fosters transparency and immutability but also enables more inclusive and equitable participation in the digital world.

Pi Network's Leadership in Web 3:

1. Decentralized and Inclusive Mining:

Pi Network's unique approach to mining sets it apart as a true Web 3 leader. Unlike traditional cryptocurrencies that require specialized hardware and high energy consumption, Pi Network allows users to mine Pi tokens through their mobile phones. This approach promotes inclusivity, as it enables individuals from all walks of life to participate in the mining process without the need for expensive equipment. By embracing millions of users globally, Pi Network has become a prime example of decentralized and democratized mining.

2. User-centric Data Ownership:

In the current Web 2 landscape, user data is often collected, stored, and monetized by large corporations, leaving individuals with little control over their digital footprint. Pi Network is committed to shifting this paradigm by putting data ownership back into the hands of users. Through its privacy-focused design, Pi Network ensures that personal information remains encrypted and is not accessed or exploited without user consent. This empowers users to maintain control over their data, making Pi Network a leader in championing user-centric data ownership in Web 3.

3. Fair Distribution and Tokenomics:

One of the critical challenges in Web 3 is achieving fair distribution of tokens and creating sustainable tokenomics. Pi Network has addressed this concern by implementing a unique invitation-based mining system during its early stages. This mechanism ensured a wide distribution of tokens among users, preventing centralization and promoting community-driven growth. By fostering a balanced and inclusive token economy, Pi Network showcases its commitment to fair distribution, a cornerstone principle of Web 3.

4. Community Governance:

Web 3 envisions decentralized governance models where community members actively participate in decision-making processes. Pi Network has embraced this concept through its user-driven approach to development and decision-making. Pioneers are encouraged to actively contribute to the network's growth, offer suggestions, and engage in discussions about Pi Network's evolution. This level of community governance is a testament to Pi Network's leadership in promoting decentralized decision-making within the Web 3 ecosystem.

Practical Examples of Pi Network's Web 3 Leadership:

1. Mass Adoption and Accessibility:

Pi Network's mobile-based mining has democratized cryptocurrency participation. Its user-friendly approach has led to widespread adoption, with millions of pioneers worldwide mining Pi on their smartphones. This accessibility and user-centric design exemplify the Web 3 vision of creating an internet for all, regardless of technical expertise or geographical location.

2. Secure and Trustworthy Transactions:

With blockchain as its backbone, Pi Network ensures secure and trustworthy transactions. The use of cryptographic principles and consensus mechanisms guarantees immutability and transparency, a vital aspect of Web 3 applications. Pi Network's commitment to data privacy and user security further reinforces its status as a leader in building a more trustworthy internet ecosystem.

3. Community-Driven Development:

Pi Network's commitment to community governance empowers pioneers to actively shape the network's future. By engaging in discussions, proposing ideas, and participating in decision-making, pioneers play a pivotal role in the development of the Pi Network. This community-driven approach aligns perfectly with the Web 3 ethos of decentralized governance and collective decision-making.

4. Empowering the Unbanked and Underserved:

By offering a mobile mining platform, Pi Network has the potential to empower the unbanked and underserved populations worldwide. Through the Pi app, users can access financial services, create a digital identity, and participate in the global economy. This financial inclusivity aligns with Web 3's vision of creating a more equitable and accessible internet for everyone.

In conclusion, Pi Network stands as a beacon of hope and innovation in the pursuit of a decentralized and inclusive internet - Web 3. Its commitment to accessible mining, user-centric data ownership, fair distribution, and community governance showcases its leadership in advancing the principles of Web 3. Through its pioneering efforts, Pi Network is actively shaping a future where the wealth of the internet is unleashed to all users, promoting empowerment, transparency, and financial inclusion for a truly decentralized world.

Chapter 14: Unleash The Power Of Networking Through Pi

Welcome to marvelous Network Marketing World Chapter, where we're about to dive into the unlimited benefits it holds for Pioneers and their mining down lines! Get ready to unleash the power of your social connections and turn them into a force to be reckoned with - just like a herd of wild cats chasing down opportunities!

Imagine you're the leader, and you're like the main cat in this marketing adventure. When you start mining Pi, you'll realize you're not alone in this journey. You'll gather a group of people, your down lines, who will also mine Pi with your help.

Think of your down lines as a team of cats working together. The more cats you have in your team, the more Pi you all get, whenever they start mining session your mining rate keeps growing. The thrilling aspect is that you get to enjoy these benefits as long as Pi is continuously mined, which will persist for decades to come. It's like everyone gets to share the treats!

But here's the cool part: as your down lines build their own teams. The pi network community keeps on growing which will have ripple effects of the value of Pi on basis of the population on the network. Your mined pi value will keep growing in years to come. It's like a chain reaction of success.

But wait, there's more! It's not just about the Pi, oh no! Network marketing is about nurturing relationships, forming bonds stronger than a cat's love for cardboard boxes. Your down lines become your feline family, and together, you embark on a journey that's more thrilling than chasing laser beams on a moonlit night.

And here's where the magic happens - you don't just teach your down lines to mine Pi; you show them how to embrace their inner lions and lionesses. You empower them to take charge of their destinies, to dream big, to conquer their fears, and to embrace their full potential. In this network of feline prowess, everyone rises together, reaching for the stars like astronauts on a cosmic catwalk!

So, my furry friends, as you unleash the power of network marketing through Pi, remember this: it's not just about the riches; it's about the roaring laughter, the shared victories, and the joy of building a community stronger than the gravitational pull of the sun.

In this whimsical world of network marketing, your down lines are not just pioneers; they are a pride of lions, and together, you create a symphony of success that echoes through the universe!

Offer Visionary and Unwavering Leadership To Your Team

As the valiant captain of your mining crew, envision yourself as the lighthouse that stands tall amidst the stormy seas. Your unwavering light shines brightly, guiding your team through any tumultuous waves of technology and application delays. Just like a beacon of hope in the darkest night, you inspire them to keep sailing forward, even when the winds of uncertainty blow.

Picture yourself as the nurturing gardener, tending to a garden of dreams and aspirations. You sprinkle seeds of encouragement and water them with optimism, cultivating a beautiful landscape of perseverance and determination. Each member of your team is a delicate bud, and with your gentle touch, you help them bloom into resilient flowers that withstand any challenges that come their way.

In the vast canvas of the mining journey, you are the artist who paints strokes of inspiration on the hearts of your companions. Your palette is filled with vibrant colors of motivation and positivity, creating a masterpiece of unity and camaraderie. Each stroke breathes life into their spirits, kindling a fire of passion that burns brighter with every setback they encounter.

As the conductor of this magnificent symphony, you orchestrate a melody of unwavering faith in the future. With every beat of your heart, you instill confidence in those who may feel disheartened, transforming doubts into unwavering belief. The harmonious notes of hope resound through the mining team, creating a symphony of resilience that echoes far beyond the challenges they face.

Through your unwavering spirit, you become the glue that holds the team together, the guiding star that leads them through the darkest nights. You infuse their hearts with the determination to press on, embracing delays as stepping stones towards greatness.

So, my steadfast leader, continue to be the lighthouse, the gardener, the artist, and the conductor. Your words of hope and encouragement are the wings that lift your team to new heights, soaring above any hurdles that may come their way. Embrace the role of inspiration and watch as your mining crew transforms into an unstoppable force, fueled by their belief in the future and supported by your steadfast leadership. Together, you will conquer any challenges and reach the shores of success, leaving a legacy of unity, resilience, and triumph for generations to come.

Guaranteed Pursive Income Through Your Strong Mining Team

Imagine your mining team as a well-tuned engine, tirelessly churning out a stream of passive income that flows steadily and abundantly for many years to come. Just like a perpetual motion machine, the efforts put in today create a never-ending cascade of rewards in the future.

Each member of your team is like a cog in this intricate machinery, working harmoniously to keep the gears turning. As they diligently mine Pi and build their own down lines, the momentum builds, and the income generated multiplies with each passing day.

It's like planting a money tree that blossoms with fruitful returns season after season. The seeds of hard work and dedication sown today sprout into a flourishing orchard of financial prosperity in the future.

And just like a wise farmer, you nurture this orchard, ensuring that it continues to bear sweet fruits for years and years.

As the leader, you provide the vision and guidance that keeps the momentum going. Your encouragement and support act as the fuel that drives this income-generating machine. Your team draws strength from your unwavering belief in the potential of Pi and the power of network marketing.

In this pursuit of passive income, your team becomes a close-knit community, bound by a shared purpose and a collective goal. Together, you embark on a journey of financial freedom, with each member contributing their unique skills and strengths, like a symphony of talents playing in perfect harmony.

Over the years, this pursuit becomes a legacy, passed down from one generation of pioneers to the next. Just like an inheritance of prosperity, the benefits of your team's efforts continue to bless the lives of those who come after you.

As time goes on, you witness the growth and transformation of your team. The passive income generated becomes a pillar of stability and security, providing a safety net for unforeseen challenges and a catalyst for dreams to become reality.

So, my visionary leader, embrace the power of this pursive income. Lead your team with unwavering determination, knowing that the seeds you plant today will bear fruit for many years to come. With each passing moment, your mining team becomes a force to be reckoned with, and the pursuit of prosperity becomes a journey that transcends time. Together, you will create a legacy of abundance, unity, and financial success that will stand the test of time.

Chapter 15: Unveiling the Hidden Gems of Pi Mining:

Embracing Boosting Strategies
In the enchanted realm of Pi Network mining, lies a secret to achieving greatness - a treasure map leading to success. The key to unlocking this treasure trove is consistency, akin to the steady rhythm of waves lapping the shore. Each day, without fail, embark on a new mining session after every 24 hours, like a seasoned adventurer setting sail for uncharted waters.

But the real gem, the crown jewel of mining, lies in embracing the art of mining boosting strategies - a path to unlocking greater rewards, like discovering a magical portal to a world of infinite possibilities.

1. The Security Circle - A Shining Fortress of Prosperity: Within this circle lies the key to network security. As you invite companions to join, each member adds to the fortress walls, fortifying it against threats. For every soul you welcome, your mining rate ascends, like an eagle soaring high on the winds of opportunity. The pinnacle of security and rewards is reached when four members stand tall together, forming a mighty shield of 100% security.

2. Lock Up Rewards - A Timeless Symphony of Abundance: Picture a majestic hourglass, each grain of sand representing a precious moment of time. The core team devised a masterful strategy - the lock up rewards - an enchanting dance between time and value. By locking up your Pi, like a butterfly pausing on a flower's petal, you unlock a bountiful reward of increased mining rate. Two parameters govern this dance: the percentage of Pi locked and the duration of its embrace. The longer the lock up,

the greater the dance of rewards. But beware, dear reader, for once you configure this enchantment, you must await the migration of mined Pi before reconfiguration.

3. Utilities Usage Bonuses - Unleashing the Magic Within: Like a curious magician exploring a book of spells, immerse yourself in the captivating applications of the Pi Network. As you interact and partake in these marvels, like a sorcerer honing their craft, your mining rate receives a boost. The very act of using these innovations conjures forth the rewards of the mystical utilities usage bonus.

4. Running Pi Node on Your Computer Bonus - A Symphony of Interconnected Nodes:

You will need stable internet connected to your computer to be able to run the node. Imagine the blockchain as a grand orchestra, where each node plays a unique instrument in harmony. To become a part of this symphony, act as the conductor of your own node. Connect your computer, like a skilled musician with their instrument, and let it join the melodic flow of success. When your Pi node is successfully accepted, like a standing ovation, you'll be rewarded with an increased mining rate, making your harmony resonate even more beautifully.

So, my fellow adventurers, take heed of these hidden gems of Pi mining. Embrace the boosting strategies like a true explorer uncovering priceless treasures. Be consistent in your pursuit, and like a constellation of stars, your mining journey will illuminate the skies of success. As you seize these strategies, the world of Pi will unveil its boundless riches, and you, dear pioneer, will stand as the epitome of prosperity and triumph.

Chapter 16: Embracing Interaction and Trade via Core Application and Community Apps

IN THE UNCHARTED TERRITORY of web 3, Pi Network pioneers the path towards a revolutionary concept. No longer shall virtual wealth be confined to the hands of a select few corporations; instead, it shall be decentralized, distributed among all users. With this profound vision in mind, the Pi Core team enthusiastically encourages developers to create applications that embody this very spirit.

Whether it's social media or any other aspect of the network, users must be duly rewarded for their contributions and interactions. The Pi Core team envisions a world where technology is demystified, making Pi accessible to the masses. Through the simplicity of a phone, anyone can partake in this exciting journey, embracing the power of the Pi ecosystem.

The Pi Network sets sail towards a horizon of inclusivity, where every pioneer plays a vital role in shaping the future. No longer shall the wealth be confined within the walls of privilege, but rather it shall flow freely, like a river nourishing the entire community. By fostering interaction and trade through core applications and community-developed apps, the Pi Network unlocks the true potential of decentralized prosperity.

As pioneers venture forth, engaging in the vibrant tapestry of interactions, they become the architects of this new digital landscape. Each post, each interaction, becomes a brushstroke on the canvas of collective growth. The rewards they reap are not just tokens, but a sense of empowerment and belonging, like the warm embrace of a close-knit community.

In this journey, technology is the vessel that carries Pi's vision across boundaries, seamlessly connecting people from all walks of life. It is the bridge that bridges the gap between the present and the future, uniting pioneers in a shared purpose. As we embark on this bold expedition, we are reminded that the true value of Pi lies not just in its token, but in the spirit of collaboration, like the harmony of a symphony.

So let us rally together, creators and users alike, forging the path towards a digital utopia. Together, we shall navigate the uncharted waters of web 3, guided by the principles of fairness, decentralization, and inclusivity. The Pi Core team invites you to join this movement, to be a part of history in the making, where virtual wealth becomes a beacon of hope for all. As we interact and trade, let us remember that the true treasure is not merely Pi, but the journey itself and the profound impact we make upon the world.

Here are some of the hackathon winners, showcasing the exciting opportunities that pioneers can seize through the mentioned applications in the Pi ecosystem:

Basic Utilities:

Pi Workforce Pool: Imagine a bustling marketplace, where skilled Pioneers come together to offer their expertise or find work opportunities. This app serves as the cornerstone of basic utilities, providing essential services for everyday life. Pioneers can connect, collaborate, and contribute their talents to various projects, fostering a thriving community of skill-sharing and productivity.

PiCare: Within this digital haven, Pioneers have a platform to report and address bugs in Pi and ecosystem apps. A crucial aspect of basic utilities, this app ensures that Pi's quality continues to soar. By collaborating and offering feedback, Pioneers actively participate in refining the ecosystem, like master artisans shaping a masterpiece.

Social Networking:

World of Pi Championships: Step into the vibrant world of a social match-three puzzle game, where Pioneers engage in friendly competitions and vie for exciting prizes. As they connect and interact, friendships blossom, and bonds are formed. The app exemplifies the essence of social networking, where Pioneers unite through playfulness, forming a global community of gaming enthusiasts.

Pi Games from Latin America:

In this heartwarming gathering, Pioneers from Latin America showcase their culture and creativity through an array of captivating games. By sharing their heritage and talent, they bridge continents and strengthen the tapestry of the Pi community. This app embodies the spirit of social networking, uniting Pioneers through the celebration of diversity.

E-Commerce:

Pi Chain Mall: A bustling digital marketplace where buyers and sellers converge, exchanging a plethora of goods and services. Pioneers embark on a shopping extravaganza, exploring a wide array of offerings. E-Commerce finds its haven here, providing a seamless shopping experience, like a grand shopping mall with endless aisles of possibilities..

Watugot: Within this marketplace, local businesses unveil their enticing coupons and discounts, captivating the hearts of eager Pioneers. This app empowers Pioneers to discover and patronize local businesses, like a treasure map leading to hidden gems. E-Commerce thrives, and local economies flourish through the support of this dynamic platform.

Enterprise:

Coinskro: Picture a secure and reliable escrow system, enabling P2P bartering of Pi for goods and services, complete with a disputes resolution mechanism. This app revolutionizes enterprise interactions, fostering trust and seamless transactions. Businesses can now trade with ease, like skilled negotiators sealing deals with a firm handshake.

Piketplace: Step into a vibrant peer-to-peer marketplace, adorned with a user-friendly interface and translations in multiple languages. Here, businesses engage in seamless transactions with fellow enterprises. This app embodies the essence of enterprise, facilitating commerce with utmost efficiency, like an advanced trading post in a bustling city.

These hackathon winners are just a glimpse of the incredible opportunities that lie within the four main categories of applications in the Pi ecosystem. The Pi Core team encourages developers to unleash their creativity, building applications that cater to the needs of the community. As pioneers seize these opportunities, the Pi platform will evolve into a realm of innovation, enhancing lives and fostering productivity across the globe. Like a garden of endless possibilities, the Pi ecosystem blossoms, thanks to the collective efforts of its passionate pioneers.

Chapter 17: Unleashing the Potential of Application Development and the Global Connection

AS THE SOARING PI RISES higher, it illuminates the sky of possibilities for developers to embark on an extraordinary journey. This vast land of opportunity beckons them to build utilities that will revolutionize lives, like seeds planted in fertile soil, sprouting into a bountiful harvest of innovation. These applications hold the power to impact not only the current 45 million Pi Network users but also the billions of people worldwide.

In this vast and unexplored terrain, developers become pioneers of change, carving a path towards a future where technology serves as a beacon of progress. They hold the key to unlocking the untapped potential of Pi, like skilled artisans shaping precious gems. With every line of code, they weave together the fabric of convenience and empowerment, crafting applications that leave an indelible mark on society.

The canvas of opportunity is vast and limitless, like an uncharted universe awaiting exploration. As developers venture forth, they discover new constellations of possibilities, illuminating the way for a better tomorrow. They become the architects of a digital landscape, designing bridges that connect people from all corners of the globe.

But the allure of this journey is not just for developers alone; existing businesses also stand at the threshold of transformation. Like a grand ballroom filled with vibrant dancers, these businesses can gracefully integrate the Pi payment feature into their existing applications. This integration is like adding a stroke of brilliance to an already mesmerizing masterpiece, enhancing the user experience and expanding the reach of their offerings.

By embracing Pi payments, businesses become part of a global movement, opening their doors to a vast network of potential customers. Like welcoming guests into a grand feast, they invite Pi users from all walks of life to partake in their offerings. This connection is not merely a transaction but a bond of trust and collaboration, like a firm handshake between friends.

The beauty of this synergy lies in its simplicity, like the gentle breeze that carries whispers of change. As developers craft innovative applications and businesses integrate Pi payments, they contribute to a world where technology serves as a catalyst for positive transformation. It's a symphony of progress, where each instrument plays in harmony, creating a melody that resonates across continents.

So, dear developers and visionary businesses, let us seize this golden opportunity. Together, we shall build utilities that change lives, like a magnificent castle rising on a hill. Let us embrace the power of Pi, like a warm embrace that unites us all. As we connect and collaborate, we sow the seeds of a brighter future, where the potential of technology knows no bounds. Let us be the storytellers of this digital age, narrating tales of progress and prosperity that echo for generations to come.

About the Author:

The author of this book is a dedicated individual who has been mining Pi consistently since 2019. With a firm belief in the potential of Pi Network and its vision for a decentralized future, the author has wholeheartedly embraced the mining process, contributing to the growth and development of the Pi community.

Over the years, the author's enthusiasm and passion for Pi have extended beyond personal mining endeavors. Recognizing the value of a strong and supportive community, the author has played a pivotal role in introducing a remarkable 1000 people to the Pi Network. By actively inviting others to join this innovative cryptocurrency platform, the author has championed the spirit of inclusivity and empowerment that Pi represents.

Through this book, the author aims to share their knowledge and experiences, shedding light on the opportunities and challenges within the cryptocurrency and blockchain space. Drawing from their firsthand involvement in Pi Network and the wider crypto community, the author provides valuable insights and perspectives that can benefit readers seeking to navigate the world of digital assets and decentralized finance.

With a deep understanding of the transformative potential of cryptocurrencies and blockchain technology, the author's expertise offers a guiding hand for those who wish to explore the world of Pi and other decentralized ecosystems. This book serves as a testament to the author's unwavering commitment to the principles of decentralization, financial empowerment, and the belief that a more inclusive and equitable financial future is within reach.

As a dedicated Pi miner and a passionate advocate for financial inclusion, the author's journey is an inspiring testament to the power of persistence, community engagement, and the boundless possibilities that lie ahead in the ever-evolving world of decentralized finance.